D1562827

THE BOOKS
OF THE
OLD TESTAMENT

THE BOOKS OF THE OLD TESTAMENT

Walter W. Stuenkel

Publishing House
St. Louis

Concordia Publishing House, St. Louis, Missouri
Copyright © 1977 Concordia Publishing House
Library of Congress Catalog Card No. 76-56246

MANUFACTURED IN THE UNITED STATES OF AMERICA

Library of Congress Cataloging in Publication Data
Stuenkel, Walter W 1912-
     The books of the Old Testament.
     "Companion volume to The books of the New Testa-
ment, edited by Herbert T. Mayer and published . . . in 1969."
     Bibliography: p.
     1.   Bible.   O.   T.—Introductions.   I.   Title.
BS1140.2.S88   221.6'7   76-56246
ISBN 0-570-03749-2

Dedicated to the several thousand students of Concordia College Milwaukee, with whom the author enjoyed the study of the Old Testament from 1953 to 1976

Contents

8

Preface

"Why another book on the Old Testament?" We can easily understand this question being raised by any clergyman or layman who is aware of the large number of studies on all or parts of the Old Testament in the last three decades. This book was produced as a companion volume to *The Books of the New Testament,* edited by Herbert T. Mayer and published by Concordia Publishing House in 1969.

Too many Christians fail to appreciate much of the richness of the New Testament revelation because they are not conversant enough with the Old Testament background which the New Testament writers take for granted in many different references and quotations.

Furthermore, the Old Testament writings are, as Paul says in 2 Tim. 3:15 f., "given by inspiration of God" and are, therefore, in themselves "able to make thee wise unto salvation through faith which is in Christ Jesus" and "profitable" for Christian living in this world. Any Christian who diligently studies the Old Testament, especially in chronological sequence as we have attempted to present it, will find it to be amazingly relevant and helpful for living in a world like ours today. Every Christian will also note that any in-depth study will expose him to the different versions of the Bible that have come into use over the years, some of them with different chapter and verse references.

We pray that every reader may find this booklet an inspiration and a guide toward the study of every book of

10

the Old Testament in its entirety and through this be led to a greater realization and appreciation of the majesty and mercy of our almighty and eternal God.

Sincere thanks are due to our colleague at Concordia College, Milwaukee, Dr. Walter A. Jennrich, for his helpful review and to Miss Ruth Loppnow, our secretary, for her careful typing of the original manuscript.

Walter W. Stuenkel

Introduction

The Old Testament has basic relevance in the life of every Christian because through it comes not only the revelation of the origin of the world in which we live but also the origin of sin and evil, how it brought down God's curse, and with it God's loving promise to free man from the dreadful results of the curse of sin. No one can properly appreciate the Old Testament who does not discover the golden thread of prophecy which assures man of the coming of the Messiah, identified in the New Testament as Jesus Christ, the Savior of the world.

In reading the Old Testament, it is necessary to be aware that it reflects cultures, customs, and conditions quite different from those which current readers have experienced. It must be recognized that the writers employ various literary forms in order to communicate the truth of God's revelation.

The Canon

One continuing set of questions raised by Bible students revolves around these topics: origin of Old Testament books, preservation of copies, determination of authentic books, and conviction regarding completeness of books retained. Obviously, this book cannot exhaustively discuss these topics but a few comments may be helpful to the lay reader. As far as can be presently determined, God's revelation was transmitted orally before it was committed to writing. In the course of time "holy men of God" were "moved by the Holy Ghost" (2

Peter 1:21) to write down what God had revealed to them, much of which they had already orally imparted to the people. The period during which the books were written stretched over centuries. Many authors of different personalities were involved.

Gradually the children of God, especially during and after the Babylonian Captivity, 606 B.C., and thereafter, began to assemble all the inspired writings into one volume. No definite information concerning the early stages of this process has been authoritatively established. There are indications of this starting in the days of Ezra and Nehemiah.

We speak of this as "canonization." The word *canon* (cane) etymologically means "a rod" or "stick" used to measure things to determine if they were up to standard. Thus the "canonical books" of the Old Testament are those books which through the years were accepted (as a group) by the church as the authentic and normative "Word of God." The Old Testament makes reference to other books, viz., "The Wars of Jehovah" and "The Book of Jashar" (Num. 21:14; Joshua 10:13; 2 Sam. 1:18), which evidently were not inspired and are nowhere to be found today. Another group of books, which Jewish scholars refused to include among the canonical books, became known as "The Apocrypha" (books of unknown origin and authenticity). These were, however, included in the best known Greek translation of the Old Testament, *Septuagint,* and in the Latin *Vulgate,* and were accepted as canonical by the Roman Catholic Church at the Council of Trent. This accounts for the fact that Roman Catholic versions of the Old Testament include 46 books, rather than 39 as in Jewish and Protestant versions.

The determination of "closing the Old Testament canon" for the Jewish community with these 39 books was made by a group of Jewish scholars in 90 A.D. at Jamnia, a small town near the Mediterranean Sea in

Judah. These scholars officially confirmed the canonicity of Judaism's Scriptures, thereby merely certifying what was already a reality through common usage and divine providence. The four major considerations for canonicity were: indications of divine character; conforming to the Torah, the Law of Moses; written before 424 B.C. (Josephus' suggestion); and written in the Hebrew language.

This did not settle the matter for all other groups. The Samaritan community in central Palestine accepted only the first six books (Genesis through Joshua) as canonical. The Alexandrian community, a large Greek-speaking Jewish group in Egypt, which had produced the Septuagint, accepted some of the "apocryphal" books as canonical. Today, more than ever before, consensus seems to be developing, especially after diligent study of the Dead Sea Scrolls since 1947, among Christian churches throughout the world toward worldwide acceptance of the canon of the standard 39 books of the Old Testament.

Theories in the Study of the Old Testament

For the last several centuries scholarly research has concerned itself far more with authorship and authenticity than with canonicity of Old Testament books. Many arguments advanced in this area have disturbed faithful Christians. They contend that the proposed solutions undermine the authority of God's Word. It should be pointed out also that many assertions of scholars are mere theories or hypotheses or suppositions for which there is no incontrovertible evidence.

Obviously, this little volume is not designed to discuss in detail all the theories of literary criticism, form criticism, or redaction criticism, but because the Old Testament is especially the object of much of this learned criticism, the issues deserve some brief comment for the benefit of the readers.

Most of the debate has centered on the composition of the Pentateuch. Men like the Dutch philosopher Spinoza (1632—1677), and later Jean Astruc (1684—1766), physician to Louis XV, began to question the Mosaic authorship because of two seemingly different accounts of creation, references to post-Mosaic conditions, and the account of Moses' death. This eventually led to the development of the theory variously referred to as the Graf-Wellhausen Theory, the Documentary Hypothesis, or the J-E-D-P Theory. Scholars are not agreed on the details, but in broad and somewhat simplistic terms this may be described as the compilation of four documents, none of which is extant, known as *J*, supposedly written about 850 B.C., especially interested in Judah and using Yahweh or Jahweh as designation of God; *E*, estimated to have been written about 750 B.C. as the "Bible of Israel," using El or Elohim as designation of God; *D* (Deuteronomy), supposed to be the document King Josiah discovered in the temple repair in 621 B.C.; and *P*, "Book of the Priests," dating from about 500 B.C., composed largely of rules for ritual and sacrifice. Those that accept this J-E-D-P Theory hold that some time after the Exile these four documents were fitted together by a Redactor (R) to form the present Pentateuch.

Bible students should seek to understand and appreciate the many contributions scholars have made in recent years to Old Testament studies through analysis of various styles of writing, through archeological discoveries, and through honest attempts to reconstruct the original circumstances prevailing in Old Testament times. All this has helped students to approach the Old Testament more realistically as living literature with Hebraic artistic forms best presenting the burden of the particular message God wanted to reveal to His people. It must be recognized that the Hebrews of the Old Testament were a minority in the total population of the Fertile Crescent, the ancient Near East, and thus information regarding the historical and cultural environment in which the Old Testament Scriptures came into existence is helpful to a better understanding of their meaning. The unique element, namely, that the Old Testament throughout is a theological document, revealing the one true God as the subject, a God, always just but also always gracious, and human life as the object, makes all reading and study of the Old Testament faith-inspiring and life-enriching. It is in that spirit that this set of outlines of all the books of the Old Testament is being presented.

Order of Books Presented

The word "Bible" is derived from the Greek word *biblia* which means "books." Thus even though the Bible is essentially one book with one final Author, the Holy Spirit, it is also an entire library of books with various human authors. In a library the books must be arranged according to some system that enables the reader to locate a specific book more readily. Various arrangements of this "library of books" have been attempted to assist the readers.

The Hebrew Old Testament was divided into three major groups: (1) Torah (Law), (2) Nebi'im (Prophets), and (3) Kethubim, Hagiographa (Sacred Writings). The *Torah* included Genesis, Exodus, Leviticus, Numbers, Deuteronomy. The *Nebi'im* were subdivided as follows: (a) the earlier prophets, including Joshua, Judges, 1 and 2 Samuel, 1 and 2 Kings; (b) the later prophets, including Isaiah, Jeremiah, Ezekiel, and the twelve minor prophets, Hosea through Malachi. The *Kethubim* or Hagiographa followed with books in this order: Psalms, Proverbs, Job, Song of Solomon, Ruth, Lamentations, Ecclesiastes, Esther, Daniel, Ezra, Nehemiah, and 1 and 2 Chronicles.

This sequence was not consistently maintained by the Jewish Talmudists and Masorites, and was changed decidedly by the Jewish scholars who prepared the

Septuagint (Greek) translation, and changed again by
Jerome in the Vulgate (Latin) translation. Most English
versions follow the sequence of the King James Version:
(1) Law: Genesis through Deuteronomy; (2) History:
Joshua through Esther; (3) Poetry: Job through Song of
Solomon; (4) Prophets: Isaiah through Malachi.

There is nothing sacred about the literary groupings
in which Old Testament books have been placed. This is
purely a matter of judgment and convenience to assist the
reader to grasp the thread of Old Testament revelation
more comprehensively and cohesively. In this book an
attempt is made to place all thirty-nine books into a
sequential historical-chronological setting, even though
much debate continues about the historical setting of
certain books as well as concerning the time of writing.
Even though many of the disputes and disagreements
have valid bases, this is still considered a helpful
approach by Bible students because the Old Testament
takes on new richness of meaning and appreciation when
individual books are considered in a chronological
sequence.

The sequence to be followed is this: (a) *Patriarchal:*
Genesis, Job; (b) *Theocracy:* Exodus, Leviticus,
Numbers, Deuteronomy, Joshua, Judges, Ruth; (c)
Monarchy: 1 Samuel, 2 Samuel, Psalms, 1 Chronicles, 1
Kings, 2 Chronicles, Proverbs, Ecclesiastes, Song of
Solomon; (d) *Divided Kingdom and Prophets:* 2 Kings,
Obadiah, Joel, Jonah, Amos, Hosea, Isaiah, Micah,
Nahum, Habakkuk, Zephaniah, Jeremiah, Lamen-
tations; (e) *Exile:* Daniel, Ezekiel; (f) *Post-Exilic:* Ezra,
Haggai, Zechariah, Esther, Nehemiah, Malachi.

This study booklet will miss its purpose if it fails to
move the reader to read the Old Testament itself in its
entirety. The reader is encouraged to read the comments
on an Old Testament book in this presentation and then
immediately to read the specific Old Testament book in
its entirety in a popular translation. There is too much

piecemeal reading of the Old Testament. No part of any book of the Bible will give the reader the satisfaction that can be gained from the whole message of the respective book. Likewise studying one book cannot possibly enrich the reader as much as a grasp of all 39 books of the Old Testament, each of which has a vital relation to all others. The careful student will find that the Old Testament in its central purpose reveals the love of God, who promised a Savior from sin and providentially led all history to "the fullness of the time" when the Savior became man. Not all questions about inspiration, canonicity, chronology, literary forms, authorship, and historicity can be answered, but the unity of thought and purpose demonstrates there is only one real Author, the Holy Spirit, and all of the Old Testament is the inspired, reliable, infallible WORD OF GOD.

1

The Patriarchal Period

Introduction

When Jesus Christ, having risen from the dead on Easter morning, walked with two men on the first Easter afternoon on their way to Emmaus and found them confused about His death and reports of His resurrection, Luke tells us that He opened unto them the Scriptures: "Beginning at Moses and all the prophets, He expounded unto them in all the Scriptures the things concerning Himself" (Luke 24:27). Later when Paul had been brought as a prisoner to Rome, he called the leaders of the Jews in Rome together "to whom he expounded and testified the kingdom of God, persuading them concerning Jesus, both out of the law of Moses, and out of the prophets, from morning till evening" (Acts 28:23).

This is the example we will follow in this brief presentation and analysis of the books of the Old Testament. We believe this is the key to a proper understanding and appreciation of God's Old Testament revelation, namely, the faith that these writings were inspired by God "to make us wise unto salvation through faith which is in Christ Jesus" (2 Tim. 3:15). Reading from that perspective, every book of the Old Testament carries a meaningful and faith-strengthening message for the reader and reduces the inclination to get lost in mere questions and problems of language and culture and authorship and chronology.

The Book of Genesis

The obvious book with which to begin this study is "the book of origins or beginnings," commonly entitled "Genesis," the Greek word for "beginning." It may be helpful to look upon this book as a brief overview or synopsis of world history, possibly written especially for the Jews to see what had transpired before their redemption from the bondage in Egypt. A greater period of history is compressed in this first book of the Old Testament than in all the remaining thirty-eight (38) put together.

During Old Testament days and for hundreds of years in New Testament times, it was assumed that Moses was the writer of Genesis as well as of the other four books of the Pentateuch (Greek word for "five scrolls") because of internal indications like Ex. 17:14; 24:4, 7; Num. 33:2; Deut. 31:9-11 and 24-26; and because of references to Moses in other places of the Old Testament like these: Joshua 8:31-33; 2 Kings 14:6; Ezra 3:2; and because of statements by Christ and others in the New Testament: Mark 12:26; Luke 24:27; Acts 7:37, 38; Rom. 10:5; Acts 28:23. Questions have been raised, however, in the last century especially, about the Mosaic authorship because of passages like the following: Gen. 14:14: "Abraham . . . pursued as far as Dan," a name not current until the time of the Judges; Gen. 36:31: "before there reigned any king over the children of Israel"; Gen. 50:10, 11; Num. 35:14; Deut. 4:46: use of the expression "beyond the Jordan"; Ex. 11:3; Num. 12:3: highly complimentary statements about Moses; and Deut. 34:5-12: account of Moses' death. This entire question of Pentateuchal authorship continues to be debated by Old Testament scholars. All theories and hypotheses, to be useful, in our opinion, must begin with the premise that through human authors the Holy Spirit was at work providentially revealing through inspiration God's Word of truth in all that was written in the Pentateuch.

This first book of the Old Testament, Genesis ("beginning"), has been referred to as "the seed book of the Bible," from which all the rest of the Bible blossoms out. Here are some of the beginnings reported in Genesis: the beginning of the created universe, 1:1; beginning of the human race, 1:26; beginning of marriage, 2:22-24; beginning of sin in man, 3:6; beginning of Messianic prophecy, 3:15; beginning of family life, 4:1-15; beginning of a man-made civilization, 4:16—9:29; beginning of nations, 11; beginning of Abraham's lineage, the chosen people of God, 12:1-3.

To appreciate Genesis and all the other books of the Old Testament properly, some elementary geographical knowledge is necessary: Cf. map. Important places are indicated to provide a frame of reference. This entire area measured less than one thousand (1,000) miles from Mt. Ararat in the north, to the Persian Gulf or the Red Sea in the south, and less than fifteen hundred (1,500) miles from Egypt and the Mediterranean Sea in the west, to the Tigris River in the east. Only one third of all this land was agriculturally productive; most of the rest consisted of desert wastes and rocky plateaus. God in His wise providence gave His people the land of Canaan or Palestine which had natural protective borders: desert on the east and south, the sea and a rocky coast on the west, and mountains to the north, and yet this land, only about 150 miles long and 50 miles wide, was the corridor through which practically all traffic of the Fertile Crescent moved from Mesopotamia to Egypt, thus giving God's people an opportunity to be a witness to the world.

In its presentation of "beginnings" Genesis teaches us much theology (study of God) and anthropology (study of man) which is amplified but never changed or contradicted by subsequent Old Testament history and literature. God reveals Himself as the Creator and Initiator. All creation owes its existence and sustenance to God. In dealing with His creation God is always sovereign, under no obligation to any individual or any people. He has, however, in love established a covenant with His chosen people, to which He will be absolutely faithful and which guarantees redemption and ultimate victory and peace to those who remain His own by faith.

Man is the crown of God's creation. With the dignity of having been made "in God's image," Gen. 1:26, man had the qualities of God except e. g., for the supreme sovereignty ("omni" element) and creative powers. Accordingly, man's life has a distinct purpose: to serve and glorify God on earth and to enjoy His presence forever in heaven. This makes sin such a disastrous tragedy, because it is rebellion against God's sovereignty and love, rejection by man of his purpose of life, and erection of a wall of separation between God and man.

In that perspective let us take a brief but comprehensive look at Genesis, "the book of beginnings." "In the beginning God created the heaven and the earth," Gen. 1:1. "And God saw everything that He had made, and, behold, it was very good," 1:31. It is a thrilling delight to read Gen. 1 and 2 and see the close intimate fellowship between God and man and woman.

Conditions change radically in Gen. 3 with the entrance of sin into the world due to man's rebellion, but hope is offered by God's broad promise of redemption in Gen. 3:15. Hereafter all people are divided into two classes: those who disregard or reject the promise and remain in rebellion and separation; and those who believe the promise and demonstrate this in serving and glorifying God, Gen. 4 and 5. As world population increased, intermarriage occurred between unbelievers and believers, Gen. 6:2; and "the wickedness of man was great in the earth," Gen. 6:5.

Only one family, Noah and his three sons and their respective wives "found grace in the eyes of the Lord" and were saved from perishing in a flood that killed all the other people on earth, Gen. 6, 7, and 8. Yet after the flood sin brought rebellion and separation into Noah's family and descendants, and degeneration started all over again so that God inflicted separation among men by "confounding their language," Gen. 9, 10, 11. Yet God's love moved Him to another "beginning," the establishment of a covenant with a descendant of one of the sons of Noah, Shem. This man's name was Abram. God promised to bless him and to make him a blessing to "all the families of the earth," Gen. 12:3.

In this covenant God pledged: (1) that Abram's descendants would be God's people; (2) that they would be numerous; (3) that Canaan would be their land; (4) that one of Abram's descendants would be the Messiah. Abram's and his people's obligations would include: (1) accepting God as the only Lord; (2) believing God's promises; (3) faithfully keeping God's commandments; and (4) accepting circumcision as the distinct sign of being separate from the other peoples of the world. Abraham's life under this covenant is described in Gen. 12—25, honestly presenting sinful weaknesses and failures as well as tremendous demonstrations of faith and loyalty to God's covenant.

After Abraham we see the covenant relationship continued with his son, Isaac, where the two elements of rebellion and separation in contrast to faith and service become quite evident again in Isaac's two sons, Esau and Jacob, Gen. 26—28. The rest of this "book of beginnings" is devoted to Jacob's life under the covenant with his large family, Gen. 29—50, with two chapters, Gen. 33 and 36, indicating the way that Esau went to found the people of Edom, south of the Dead Sea.

These chapters of Genesis relating the story of Jacob are a marvelous picture of the overwhelming forgiving love of God, as the Messianic promise is passed on from Jacob to his son Judah, Gen. 49:10, and not to his son Joseph, who is a great type of Christ, Gen. 39—50. Joseph moves from dreams through dungeons to diadems as a loyal son of his father and becomes responsible for Jacob's entire family's finding a safe haven in the land of Goshen in Egypt in the delta of the Nile River.

The Book of Job

No one knows exactly when Job lived. Many scholars maintain that Job never lived but that this book is an inspired poem using fictitious characters to emphasize important truths. Tennyson called it "the greatest poem, whether of ancient or modern literature." This high quality of poetry leads many scholars to place the time of writing in "the Golden Age" of Hebrew poetry and to consider Solomon the author. Others set the date of writing much later and others much earlier.

Those that hold that Job is a historic personality quote Ezek. 14 where in v. 14 and again in v. 20 Job is mentioned as a righteous man together with Noah and Daniel. They also refer to James 5:11 where we read, "Ye have heard of the patience of Job." Some of the reasons supporting the placing of this story in the patriarchal period are these: (1) names like Uz, Buz, Shuah in Job 1:1; 32:2; 8:1 relate to Gen. 22:21 and Gen. 25:2; (2) Job's great age, Job 42:16; (3) the practice of sacrifices, cf. Job 1:5 and Job 42:8 with Gen. 22:13; Gen. 31:54; and Gen. 46:1; (4) the fact that this area and its people are still regarded favorably by God whereas after Numbers this land which is Edom is under God's curse.

The book can be easily divided into four sections: Prolog, Job 1—3; Dialogs, Job 4—26; Monologs, Job 27—41; Epilog, Job 42. The prolog and epilog are prose and the dialogs and monologs are poetry. We believe the book fits well with Genesis since its message deals with the character of man's relationship to God and vividly illustrates the tension that constantly exists even in people of the covenant between living trustingly and gratefully in God's grace and living by a system of rewards and punishments because of one's deeds. Job espoused the former and his "friends" the latter. Under the pressure of continuous confrontation from his "friends," even Job began to falter in his relationship to God and His grace until God personally began to speak. Then Job repented, the loving covenant relationship was restored, and Job was abundantly blessed.

In the prolog, Job 1—3, we see the intimate relationship between God and Job challenged by the intervention of the devil, assisted by Job's wife and Job's friends. The dialogs, Job 4—26, present the charges of each of the three "friends," Eliphaz, Bildad, and Zophar, and Job's response in three sections: Job 4—14, attitude toward God vitiated by an overemphasis on God's justice; Job 15—21, the "friends'" formula: man sins, God punishes, man suffers; Job 22—26, another formula of the "friends": great affliction is always the result of great sinning. Job's most eloquent response is Job 19:23-27, where he confidently asserts that at some future date, his Goel (Redeemer), which is God, will arise and vindicate Job. Christian scholars have through the centuries referred this dramatic statement of Job to the glorious resurrection on Easter morning of Jesus Christ, the world's "Goel."

Job, however, becomes impatient that vindication is so slow in coming, that he strains the relationship with God by challenging God's sovereignty in the first monolog, Job 27—31. A young man, Elihu, unsuccessfully tries to arbitrate in the second monolog, Job 32—37. Then follows the third monolog, Job 38—41, by God Himself, one of the most majestic presentations of God's sovereignty in all of Scripture. This leads to the epilog, Job 42, with the intimate relationship between Job and God restored, involving Job's repentance and God's abundant blessing expressed in the names of the daughters: Jemima, "sunshine" for sorrow; Kezia, "fragrant spice" for the smell of boils; Keren-happuch; "plenty restored" after all had been taken away. What helpful instruction this book might have been for God's people in their trek through the wilderness and their relationship with God thereafter under the theocracy!

2

The Period of the Theocracy

The Book of Exodus

Genesis takes us from Adam to Joseph and from the Garden of Eden, evidently somewhere in the Mesopotamian area near the Tigris and Euphrates rivers, to Egypt dominated by the Nile. The kingdom of Egypt had already existed for over a thousand (1,000) years and had already been ruled by twelve dynasties before Joseph arrived there. The great pyramids, the only remainders today of the seven great wonders of the ancient world, were already hundreds of years old. A group of foreign rulers, non-Egyptians known as Hyksos, were in control which made it possible for a non-Egyptian like Joseph to rise to such a prominent position of power.

But after Joseph's death and several hundred years before Moses was born, Egyptian leaders drove the Hyksos out and also gained control of Palestine. Such was the situation as the Book of Exodus begins. The Egyptian Pharaoh was happy to have the Hebrews (possibly from *habiru* which means "wanderer, nomad, foreigner") serve as slaves, but he was always suspicious, because of the Hyksos history, that they might rise in rebellion, Ex. 1:10. The Book of Exodus presents God's deliverance of His people from the tyranny of the Egyptian Pharaoh and the formal establishment of the covenant with these descendants of Abraham, Isaac, and Jacob. We may divide the book into three parts: Ex 1—12, in Egypt, Revelation; Ex. 13—18 on the way to Mt. Sinai, Redemption; Ex. 19—40, at Mt. Sinai, Response. The major character is Moses, whose life can be divided into three 40-year periods: Ex. 1:1-2, 15: Moses' birth and life to age 40 in Egypt; Ex. 2:16—4:31: Moses' exile in Midian near Mt. Sinai to age 80; Ex. 5:1— Deut. 34:12: Moses' leadership of God's people from Egypt to Mt. Nebo to age 120.

God's gracious providence is emphasized at the very beginning of Exodus in saving Moses' life through Pharaoh's daughter, Ex. 1 and 2, then through Moses being welcomed into the household of Jethro, the Midian priest, whose daughter, Zipporah, becomes Moses' wife, Ex. 2:16 ff. God's call to Moses in chapter 3 leads to the revelation of His covenant name, *Jahweh,* a Hebrew term which reveals God as the Eternal, the Independent, Initiating Lord of the Covenant, "I AM THAT I AM." The Jews were so afraid of misusing this name that they used the substitute word *Adonai,* which means "Lord." Later by mistake the vowels of Adonai were placed with the consonants of Jahweh which formed the word "Jehovah."

In faith in Jahweh Moses returned to Egypt and demonstrated God's power over even a mighty Pharaoh through ten plagues, Ex. 4—11. This climaxed with the death of the firstborn in every Egyptian home, while the angel of death "passed over" the houses of God's people marked with "the blood of a lamb," an occasion forever after to be celebrated as the Passover Festival, Ex. 12:1— 13:16.

This tragic experience led the Pharaoh to order Moses to lead God's people out of Egypt. Even though the destination was Palestine, Moses did not lead the people north as would be expected, Ex. 13:17, but south where they had to cross a body of water (not the Red Sea which is still farther south, cf. map, but the Reed Sea) where Pharaoh tried to overtake them, but God miraculously delivered His people, Ex. 13:18—15:21.

Even with these great evidences of God's providence and redemption, His people murmured when they encountered other difficulties on their journey to Mt. Sinai, Ex. 15:22—18:27.

After two months of traveling, this mighty multitude of more than a million people arrived at Mt. Sinai, and God reminded them of His providence and proposed a covenant of love, Ex. 19:3-6. The people gave a unanimous positive response, Ex. 19:7-9. This may well be regarded as the climactic point in the entire Old Testament. Thereupon God made covenant arrangements in greater detail, e. g., Ten Commandments, Ex. 20; further explanations, Ex. 21—24; and construction patterns for the tabernacle, Ex. 25—31.

With such positive demonstration of God's love one would expect His people to continue to respond in grateful service. But because Moses did not return from Mt. Sinai as promptly as the people expected, they requested Aaron, Moses' brother, to build them an idol and Aaron acquiesced, Ex. 32:1-6. God became very angry, but Moses interceded and pleaded for mercy even though he severely remonstrated with the people, Ex. 32:7—33:17. Because the tribe of Levi stood by Moses in this crisis, God announced that all priests and servants in worship and sacrifice would henceforth be selected from this tribe, Ex. 32:25-28; cf. also Lev. 8—10. Thereupon God gave special revelations of His glory to Moses so that Moses' face shone as he came down from Mt. Sinai the second time, Ex. 33:18—34:35.

This time the people responded willingly with an abundance of gifts of jewelry and gold toward the construction of the tabernacle, Ex. 35. Two gifted men, Bezaleel and Aholiab, supervised the construction which God had prescribed in great detail, Ex. 36—40. God was pleased and indicated His presence by a cloud that covered the tabernacle every day. Thus ends the Book of Exodus.

The Book of Leviticus

As the name "Exodus" ("the way out") indicates that the Book of Exodus tells about God's people on their way out of Egypt, so the name "Leviticus" ("Levites") tells us that in the Book of Leviticus we will learn about the duties and obligations of the people in their worship life, led by the Levites. This follows naturally after the account of the construction of the tabernacle, the place for worship and sacrifice, in the last chapters of Exodus. There are three sections in the Book of Leviticus: directions for sacrifices, Lev. 1—10; discipline procedures, Lev. 11—22; and laws for worship and special festivals, Lev. 23—27. Because the relation between God and His people is a theocracy ("direct rule by God"), Leviticus gives us not only moral laws, which count for all people for all time, but also many ceremonial (church) and political (civic) laws that applied only to these Old Testament people because they had only "a shadow of things to come," whereas in the New Testament we have the fulfillment in Christ, Col. 2:16, 17.

Under the direction for sacrifices, we have burnt offerings indicating self-dedication to God, Lev. 1; cereal offerings expressing thanks for physical blessings, Lev. 2; peace offerings of animals to express a loving relation to God, Lev. 3; the sin offering symbolizing the general need for atonement, Lev. 4; and the trespass offering for very serious sins, Lev. 5; in addition to general rules for sacrifices, Lev. 6 and 7. Because the priests were the only ones authorized to execute the sacrifices, careful prescriptions for the priesthood are given, Lev. 8—9. There is an example of severe punishment for those like Nadab and Abihu, sons of Aaron, who violated these prescriptions, Lev. 10.

The second section of Leviticus deals with discipline, defining clean animals (split hoofs and chewing cud), Lev. 11; rules about birth of children, Lev. 12;

leprosy, Lev. 13 and 14; and relations of men and women, Lev. 15. Then as a climax of this section the Day of Atonement (Yom Kippur) is outlined in great detail, and we see the central significance of blood in the life of God's people because of its symbolism in atonement, Lev. 16 and 17. The section concludes with rules of general discipline for the laity, Lev. 18—20, and for the clergy, Lev. 21—22.

The third section of Leviticus presents the special festivals to be observed in the worship life of God's people; Passover, Lev. 23:1-8; Pentecost, Lev. 23:9-22; the seventh month festivals: Trumpets, Atonement, and Tabernacles, Lev. 23:23-44. In the next chapter (24) God reveals the seriousness of any offense in the stoning of Shelomith's son. God wanted His people always to remember that all land belonged to Him and the people were His stewards, so He instituted laws concerning sabbath and jubilee years, and laws concerning tithing, Lev. 25—27. Leviticus concludes with the summary statement: "These are the commandments which the Lord commanded Moses for the children of Israel at Mt. Sinai," Lev. 27:34.

The Book of Numbers

It was now about thirteen months since God had led His people out of Egypt. They were now ready after the covenant instructions in Exodus and Leviticus to resume their journey to the Promised Land. Before they were to start, God wanted an accurate "numbering" by tribes of all the men, twenty years and older, Num. 1—2. This is the reason this book carries the title, "Numbers." Special attention was given to the tribe of Levi because of their spiritual duties and duties in connection with the tabernacle, Num. 3—4. God was intent that His people should not tolerate any unclean people in their midst, Num. 5, but give recognition to those who show special dedication, like the Nazarites, Num. 6. At the end of this chapter we also have the precious Aaronic blessing still used regularly in worship services today, Num. 6:24-27.

As a kind of summary or wrap-up just before the journey begins, God gives recognition to people who have rendered loyal service, Num. 7, and gives a few more final directions, Num. 8 and 9. Now all is in readiness on the twentieth day of the second month of the second year, a little over a year since they left Egypt. God prescribed the lineup for the tribes: Judah, Zebulon, Issachar in front; Dan, Asher, Naphtali on one side; Reuben, Gad, Simeon on the other side; and Ephraim, Manasseh, Benjamin in the rear. The Levites carried the tabernacle in the center, Num. 10.

The journey, no doubt, started on a high note of anticipation but very early complaints and rebellion and lust became evident again, Num. 11. Even Moses' brother and sister, Aaron and Miriam, expressed jealousy for which Miriam was stricken with leprosy, Num. 12. When they arrived at Kadesh-barnea (cf. map), which was to be their general headquarters for the next 38 years, although they did not know it at this time, Moses selected one leader from each of the tribes to visit the Promised Land as spies and bring back a report. Because of a negative report by ten of the spies, the people wished themselves back in Egypt. God was disgusted and wanted to destroy them all, but Moses pleaded for sparing them. God listened to Moses' prayer but announced that Joshua and Caleb, the two positive spies, would be the only men of Israel twenty years of age or older who had left Egypt and would enter the Promised Land, Num. 13 and 14.

Hereafter the remaining chapters of Numbers record one sad experience after another: man killed for gathering sticks on the Sabbath, Num. 15; rebellion of Korah and other Levites, 16; jealousy against Aaron, 17; portions assigned to the priests and Levites, 18 and 19; Moses' smiting the rock and losing the privilege of entering the Promised Land, 20; the snakes killing the people until Moses raises the brazen serpent, 21; the battles against Moab and Ammon, 22 and 23, with, however, a great Messianic prophecy from the heathen prophet Balaam, 24:17.

God's people disgraced God's name by committing adultery and idolatry with the Moabites and Midianites, so that God smote them with a plague in which 24,000 died, Num. 25. Now they had arrived near Mt. Nebo on the east side of the Dead Sea (cf. map), and God once more commanded a "numbering" of the people, 26. Seven tribes were larger than when they left Mt. Sinai, five were smaller, and the total number was less.

Num. 27 has two interesting and meaningful accounts: the first is the plea of the daughters of Zelophehad for an inheritance because their father died and they had no brothers; the second the heartrending announcement to Moses that he would not enter the Promised Land and that he should appoint Joshua as his successor. In Num. 28—30 God once more impressed upon His people the importance of their sacrifices, their offerings, and their vows. In Num. 31 we see good evidence that God does not forget to punish the evildoer (cf. Num. 25:16, 17).

Moses was faced with a serious dilemma when the tribes of Reuben and Gad and half of the tribe of Manasseh requested land outside the Promised Land on the east side of the Jordan. The request was granted when they promised first to help conquer the land on the west side, Num. 32. Now in final preparation for entrance into the Promised Land we have a beautiful review of the entire wilderness journey, Num. 33; the defining of the borders of the Promised Land, Num. 34; arrangement for cities for the Levites and for "cities of refuge," Num. 35; and safeguards in administration of the promise made to the daughters of Zelophehad, Num. 36.

The Book of Numbers ends with the summary statement: "These are the commandments and the judgments, which the Lord commanded by the hand of

Moses unto the children of Israel in the plains of Moab by
Jordan near Jericho," Num. 36:13.

The Book of Deuteronomy

The name "Deuteronomy" (*deuteros:* "second" and
nomos: "law") tells us that in this book we may expect to
find a review or recapitulation of the Law which God
first gave to His people at Mt. Sinai. The time is forty
years later, and we are now at Mt. Nebo or Mt. Pisgah.
Moses is 120 years old but "his eye is not dim, nor his
natural force abated," Deut. 34:7. God has told Moses that
he cannot enter the Promised Land but has given him the
opportunity to view the land from the top of Mt. Nebo.

Moses reflects no bitterness or disappointment. His
one great concern is that God's people will make the most
of the great opportunities before them. Moses, therefore,
preaches four sermons and then concludes with a
beautiful poem. Each of his messages has an element of
reminiscence, of exposition of God's law, and of
exhortation to God's people.

The theme of his first message is, "There is only one
God." This God brought His people thus far, and He
will continue to be faithful to His covenant, Deut. 1—4.
In the second address Moses emphasizes that this one God
deserves the total allegiance of His people: in the moral
law, Deut. 5—11; in ceremonial laws, Deut. 12—16; and
in political laws, Deut. 17—26. In this sermon he gives
them the words which are still memorized by Jews today,
"Hear, O Israel, the Lord our God is one Lord," Deut.
6:4; also the indication that some day the theocracy will
be replaced by kings ruling, Deut. 17:14-20; and a
Messianic prophecy, Deut. 18:15-19. Here we also find the
three texts Jesus used to stand up against the devil in His
temptation, Deut. 8:3; 6:16; and 6:13-14.

In the third message Moses instructs the people to do
what they actually carried out later (cf. Joshua 8:32-35),
namely to have six tribes on Mt. Ebal (cf. map) announce

curses upon disobedience and six tribes on Mt. Gerizim
(cf. map) announce blessings on those that keep the Law
of God, Deut. 27—28. Then in the fourth sermon Moses
called the people to a renewal of the covenant with three
challenges: trust God, don't question His ways, Deut. 29;
when you fall into sin, return to God in sincere
repentance, Deut. 30:1-3; and remain faithful to God's
Word, Deut. 30:4-20.

The next three chapters are words of strong
encouragement: the Lord is with you, fear not, Deut. 31;
God is the Rock of your salvation, build on Him, and you
are secure, Deut. 32; God has a blessing for all of you,
Deut. 33. The last chapter is an account of Moses' death,
Deut. 34.

Scholars have differing views concerning the
authorship of the Book of Deuteronomy. Traditionally
Moses is regarded as the writer with the explanation that
the events of the last chapter were revealed to him by God
before he died or that this chapter was written by an
anonymous contemporary under the inspiration of the
Holy Spirit. The scholars who subscribe to the J-E-D-P
documentary hypothesis usually label Deuteronomy as
the D document. Many assume that this was the book
which Hilkiah found in repairing the temple and which
King Josiah had the prophetess Huldah examine for
authenticity (cf. 2 Chron. 34:14-33). The last chapter has
also raised many questions about the death and burial of
Moses. Most important is the message of Deuteronomy
for all people of all time: "There is only one God. He is
faithful to His Word. Faithfulness to Him and His Word
will unfailingly result in blessings. Disobedience and
rebellion, however, will draw God's punishment and
curse."

The Book of Joshua

All the addresses of Moses in the Book of
Deuteronomy carry the tone of anticipation. During the

forty years of wilderness wanderings after leaving Egypt, the hope of the Promised Land was constantly emphasized. God's people were eager to begin to enjoy the blessings guaranteed to them by the covenant after crossing the Jordan. Moses could not accompany them. God had selected Joshua as the next leader, and Moses "laid his hands upon him, and gave him a charge, as the Lord commanded by the hand of Moses," Num. 27:23. Cf. also Deut. 34:9. Thus God provided for continuity of human leadership under the theocracy even before Moses died. After Moses had delivered his farewell messages and had viewed the land of Palestine from the top of Mt. Nebo, he died "according to the Word of the Lord," Deut. 34:5, "and the children of Israel wept for Moses in the plains of Moab thirty days," Deut. 34:8.

There the Book of Joshua begins with these words: "Now after the death of Moses, the servant of the Lord, it came to pass, that the Lord spake unto Joshua," Joshua 1:1. Because of this close connection with Deuteronomy, some scholars hold that the Book of Joshua was originally combined with the five books of the Pentateuch, and they refer to the six books as the Hexateuch, and some find indications of support for their theory of composite authorship as represented in the Documentary Hypothesis (JEDP). Other scholars name Joshua as the author because of the statement in Joshua 24:26, and some have mentioned Samuel as the writer. No evidence is definite enough to make a firm determination regarding authorship, but the Jews clearly separated this book from the previous ones by placing it in the second major grouping of the canon, namely, as the first of the Nebi'im (Prophets). It has, therefore, always been accepted by Jews and Christians alike as God's inspired account of how the people of God possessed the Promised Land. Its canonicity has not been questioned.

Palestine at this time was a highly developed land, occupied by a number of different tribes who were separated from one another not only by the geographical terrain but also by total absence of any centralized government and of any common ideology. For many years Egypt had exercised some control; but about a hundred years before this a Pharaoh of Egypt, Akhnaton, as the Amarna archeological findings have revealed, became so interested in establishing the worship of Aton, the sun-god, in Egypt that he yielded control of Palestine to individual tribes like the Canaanites, Perizzites, Hittites, and Girgashites in the northern parts of Palestine; the Hivites (Gibeonites) and Jebusites in the central area; the Philistines along the Mediterranean coast; and the Edomites, Amalekites, Midianites, and Amorites in the southern parts. These tribes were jealous of one another and thus presented no united front against the approach of God's people.

The children of Israel, having spent forty years in the bleak wilderness, were overawed by the social, physical, and agricultural development they found in Palestine. The crafts were flourishing. People were making their own weapons, tools, and pottery. Massive walls surrounded some of the cities, inside of which were strong, well-constructed buildings. Agriculturally it was "a land flowing with milk and honey," large flocks of sheep and goats were grazing in fields and on hilly slopes; vineyards and olive orchards were producing luscious fruit. All this was to become a serious temptation to God's people because they would be told by these heathen tribes that their gods made the land so productive and fertile. This belief was reflected in their idolatrous and adulterous worship practices which the children of Israel would be invited to adapt and adopt.

God knew all this and, therefore, inspired Moses to emphasize allegiance to the one true God and faithfulness to the Covenant in his farewell addresses. Now God told Joshua the same, "Only be thou strong and very courageous, that thou mayest observe to do according to all the law, which Moses, My servant, commanded thee; turn not from it to the right hand or to the left, that thou mayest prosper whithersoever thou goest," Joshua 1:7. In what manner and to what extent Joshua followed these instructions and what the results were are related in this Book of Joshua in three major divisions: the conquest to possess the land, Joshua 1—13; the division of the land and assignment to respective tribes of Israel, Joshua 14—22; Joshua's farewell messages to the people, Joshua 23—24.

As Joshua had been a spy 38 years before this (cf. Num 13:8), so now he sent two spies with instructions, "Go view the land, even Jericho," Joshua 2:1. This leads to the remarkable story of Rahab and her assistance. Having heard the positive report of the spies, Joshua prepared the people for the march across the Jordan River by emphasizing the symbolic importance of the Ark of the Covenant, Joshua 3. It was such a memorable occasion that representatives of all the tribes were instructed to erect stone monuments in the Jordan and on the bank of the Jordan to commemorate the crossing, Joshua 4. Three important events in Joshua 5 indicate the beginning of a new era for God's people: circumcision of all the males, celebration of the Passover, and cessation of the daily supply of manna.

Now the children of Israel were ready for their first great test of doing what God directed them to do in possession of the land: the conquest of Jericho, Joshua 6. An interesting example of the exactness of God in prophecy and fulfillment is found by comparing Joshua 6:26 with 1 Kings 16:34, in rebuilding Jericho. God also emphatically demonstrated the importance of complete obedience in the revelation and punishment of Achan, Joshua 7. As soon as this offense was removed, Joshua successfully conquered Ai, Joshua 8, and the Gibeonites became "hewers of wood and drawers of water" for the children of Israel, Joshua 9.

Having thus penetrated the central portion of Palestine, Joshua faced the kings of the south, "and all these kings and their land did Joshua take at one time," Joshua 10:42. Next Joshua marched to the north as far as Hazor and overcame that area also, Joshua 11—12. Even though Joshua had diligently worked and warred, God told him "there remaineth yet very much land to be possessed," Joshua 13:1; and He gave Joshua instructions how to assign the land to various tribes to finish the work, Joshua 13:7 ff.

In Gen. 49 we read of Jacob blessing his sons and indicating what part of Palestine each would inherit, and in Deut. 33 Moses gives similar indications, all of which are realized in Joshua 14—22: the inheritance of Judah, 14 and 15; of the sons of Joseph, Manasseh and Ephraim, 16 and 17; of Benjamin, 18; of Simeon, Zebulon, Issachar, Asher, Naphtali, and Dan, 19. The cities of refuge are designated, 20, and the cities for the Levites, 21. Finally, arrangements were also made for the tribes of Reuben and Gad and half of the tribe of Manasseh on the east side of the Jordan, 22.

The last two chapters of the Book of Joshua (23 and 24) remind the reader of the Book of Deuteronomy. Here Joshua at Shechem (cf. map) does just before his death at the age of 110 years what Moses had done at Mt. Nebo just before his death at the age of 120 years. He reviews God's gracious providence to His people, urges them to faithfulness, pledges himself and his family to serve the Lord (24:15), and elicits the strong positive response from the people, "The Lord our God will we serve, and His voice will we obey," 24:24. The book ends with an account of three burials: Joshua; the bones of Joseph; and Eleazar, the son of Aaron, 24:29-33.

The Book of Judges

The Book of Judges connects very directly with the Book of Joshua with its very first words, "Now after the death of Joshua it came to pass," Judges 1:1. It provides the bridge from the theocracy to the hierocracy (rule of religious leaders) and to the monarchy depicted in 1 Samuel. Some scholars regard Samuel as the writer, as does the Jewish Talmud, but no authoritative judgment can be made in reference to authorship since no definite information regarding this is available. The canonicity has, however, always been accepted by both Jews and Christians.

The book can be divided as follows: general outline of this period, Judges 1—2; the accounts of individual "judges" or "charismatic leaders" (a more appropriate term because of the expression "the Spirit of the Lord was upon him"), usually following the fivefold cycle of R's: rebellion, retribution, repentance, rescue, rest, Judges 3—16; characteristic cases of idolatry, Judges 17—18, and of adultery, Judges 19—21.

The political arrangement of this period resembled the amphictyonies (tribes loosely bound together by common religious obligations) of the early Greek peoples. The children of Israel were bound together by the covenant of God symbolized by the tabernacle and the Ark of the Covenant at Shiloh. To this they had all pledged themselves just before the death of Joshua.

But now came the struggle between faithfulness to God and His covenant and temptation to advantages which Canaanite culture seemed to offer. God bade them to make *cherem* (Deut. 7:2; 20:17) of all Canaanite culture and people by utter destruction of the same; but the children of Israel refused to do this, Judges 1—2.

God told them that as a result these Canaanite people would be "as thorns in your sides and their gods shall be a snare unto you," Judges 2:3. This lays the background for the rest of the book. Yet God in His grace did not utterly forsake His people but selected individuals, to whom He gave special charismatic gifts, to bring relief to the children of Israel when they repented.

No accurate chronology can be determined because some of these "charismatic leaders" served concurrently. They were the following: Othniel, Judges 3:7-11; Ehud, 3:12-30; Shamgar, 3:31; Deborah (the only woman listed) and Barak, 4 and 5; Gideon, 6, 7, 8; Abimelech, 9; Tola, 10:1-2; Jair, 10:3-5; Jephthah, 10:6—12:7; Ibzan, 12:8-10; Elon, 12:11-12; Abdon, 12:13-15; Samson, 13, 14, 15, 16. Some of these misused their gifts and turned virtue into vice. The ever-present desire to be "like the nations," especially in substituting "kings" for the theocracy, is evident in the request to Gideon, 8:22. Gideon emphasized the theocracy, 8:23, but one of his sons, Abimelech, ambitiously made an abortive attempt to establish a monarchy, 9.

Conditions continued to degenerate, and the reason may well be found in evil situational ethics described in Judges 17:6: "Every man did that which was right in his own eyes." Judges 17—21 give two dramatic demonstrations of this: the first (17—18) presents Micah, who is a thief and an idolater, and the tribe of Dan and its moving north; the second (19—21) tells the revolting story of adultery by the children of Benjamin and the dreadful results. The book closes with the ominous words quoted above: "Every man did that which was right in his own eyes," 21:25.

The Book of Ruth

The opening words, "Now it came to pass in the days when the judges ruled," Ruth 1:1, not only indicate the historicity of this story but also the time period when it occurred. Scholars differ widely, however, in reference to this book. The Hebrew Scriptures placed it in the third major division (Kethubim or Hagiographa) as one of the five scrolls (Megilloth) to be read on distinctive festivals. The Book of Ruth was designated for the Feast of Weeks or Pentecost, most likely because of its harvest emphasis. The Septuagint and the Vulgate placed it between Judges and Samuel evidently because it fit here historically. Josephus also seems to have regarded it as a supplement to the Book of Judges. Nothing definite can be stated about authorship. The Talmud names Samuel as the author, others have thought it was David. The canonicity has not been questioned.

These are some of the widely varying opinions by various scholars: "probably written in order to identify Ruth as the great-grandmother of David (Ruth 4:17) and thus a forbear of Jesus"; . . . "a subtle piece of 'propaganda' against the view that one's position within Israel was dependent upon purity of blood or correctness of genealogy"; . . . "portrayal of the piety of this Moabite woman"; . . . "seeks to combat the narrowness of outlook found in the books of Nehemiah and Ezra"; . . . "a beautiful idyllic epic"; . . . "offers simple historical truth"; . . . "an excellent short story or novella, ranking in quality and power with the Book of Jonah."

To us the Book of Ruth is a delightful story of God's gracious and unfailing providence toward a Jewish woman and a Gentile girl who were loyal to God at a time of general apostasy and loose morals. A simple outline of the Book of Ruth: Chapter 1, Ruth comes to Bethlehem; 2, Ruth meets a man in Bethlehem; 3, Ruth woos this man of Bethlehem; 4, Ruth wins this man of Bethlehem.

A famine in Judah drove Elimelech and his wife, Naomi, and their two sons, Mahlon and Chilion, to emigrate to Moab (cf. map). Both sons married Moabitish girls; Mahlon married Ruth, and Chilion married Orpah, Ruth 4:10. After all three men died, the three widows decided to go back to Bethlehem. On the way Orpah changed her mind and returned to Moab, but Ruth came with Naomi to Bethlehem, Ruth 1:6-22. Note her famous pledge of loyalty, Ruth 1:16-17.

Naomi was aware of the law of the gleaners, Lev. 19:9,10; Deut. 24:19, and encouraged Ruth to take advantage of this privilege. Providentially Ruth was led to glean in the field of Boaz, a relative of her deceased husband, Mahlon, Ruth 2:1-23. Naomi called Ruth's attention to another Jewish law, the law of the levirate, Deut. 25:5; Lev. 25:25, whereby the nearest eligible relative would have to serve as a *goel* ("redeemer") to the widow of a man (e.g., Mahlon) who died childless. Ruth broached this matter very modestly but forthrightly to Boaz and received a favorable response, Ruth 3:1-18. After investigating and meeting all legal requirements, Boaz married Ruth; and a son, Obed, was born to them. The last sentence of the book shows Ruth to be an ancestress of David: "Obed begat Jesse and Jesse begat David," 4:1-22, and thus also of Jesus Christ, Matt. 1:5; Luke 3:32. It is fitting and comforting that the Savior of all men should be a descendant of this Gentile woman, and that this beautiful instance of love and covenant loyalty should occur at a time in Israel's history when one might least expect it to happen.

3

The Monarchy

The First Book of Samuel

The last of the "charismatic leaders" in the Book of Judges was Samson, Judges 13—16, and the major "thorns in the side" for the children of Israel at that time were the Philistines. They had originally lived on the Island of Crete; but during the Aegean upheaval, when enemies from southern Europe had swept down upon them, the Philistines first tried to settle in Egypt. When that proved unsuccessful, they established a beachhead on the Mediterranean Coast directly west of the Dead Sea (cf. map). They were a powerful people, especially also because they were skillful in making and using weapons and instruments of iron, in fact virtually held a monopoly in iron as we learn from 1 Sam. 13:19-22. Samson had gained some victories against them but had also suffered serious defeats. Bitter hostility existed which posed a constant threat to the children of Israel.

Such was the situation as the First Book of Samuel begins. Evidently because this book and those immediately following relate the establishment and development of kings in Israel, these books (1 and 2 Samuel, 1 and 2 Kings) originally were known as the Books of the Kings. In the Septuagint the translators called 1 and 2 Samuel The First and Second Books of Kingdoms; the two books of Kings were called The Third and Fourth Books of Kingdoms. In the Vulgate the word "Kingdom" was changed to "Kings." Because Samuel represented the transition from "judges" to "kings" (since he was the last of the "charismatic leaders" and the one to anoint the first two kings), the first two of these books received their names in honor of him. No one knows who wrote these books and so many theories of authorship have been suggested. The important matter is that the divine inspiration and the canonicity of these books are corroborated by references in many of the psalms: Pss. 3, 7, 30, 34, 51, 52, 54, 56, 57, 59, 60, 63, 142, in which references are made to the life of David as reported in these books of Samuel. David's psalm in 2 Sam. 22 is repeated in Ps. 18. The following New Testament references are also significant: cf. Heb. 1:5 and 2 Sam. 7:14; Matt. 12:3-4 and 1 Sam. 21:2-6; Acts 7:46 and 2 Sam 7:2.

A very brief and broad outline of 1 Samuel could well be related to the major personalities: Samuel, 1—8; Saul, 9—15; David and Saul, 16—31. God's people were chafing more and more under the theocracy. As they had absorbed much of the Canaanite "naturalism" (imitating idolatry to gain land fertility), so they were intrigued by Canaanite "nationalism" (a monarch between them and God). It seems that for the present, however, they were content with a "hierocracy" (priest as ruler). The incumbent priest in charge of the tabernacle at Shiloh was a mild-mannered, easy-going individual by the name of Eli. The priesthood, nevertheless, was the one unifying influence among the tribes of Israel, but it was being corrupted by the wicked practices of the sons of Eli, 1 Sam. 2:12-36.

God saw all this happening and provided the way for a spiritual reformation through His answer to the fervent prayer of Hannah for motherhood, 1 Sam. 1. Hannah gave the child the name "Samuel" ("asked of God"). The account of his physical and spiritual development in these adverse circumstances, 3:1, is heartwarming and inspiring, 2—3. The depth of the degradation of the sons of Eli is demonstrated by their attempting to "force" God to go to battle with them against the Philistines by their carrying the Ark of the Covenant out of the tabernacle to the battlefield. The children of Israel not only lost the battle, but Eli's sons were killed and, hearing the report, Eli died. The Philistines captured the Ark of the Covenant and took it with them. It, however, was the cause of serious problems among the Philistines so they sent it back, 4—6, to a temporary place in Kirjathjearim. Shiloh had been completely destroyed (cf. Jer. 7:12-14 and Jer. 26:6, 9).

God now chose Samuel, not so much as a priest (he was a descendant of the non-priestly line of Levites, 1 Chron. 6:22-28, i.e., other than through the four sons of Aaron) but as a "judge" or "charismatic leader." Samuel was not a military leader but a spiritual teacher, and the people responded to his instructions, 1 Sam. 7:1-6. Once again the Philistines came to conquer, but God miraculously delivered His people, and Samuel called the memorial stone Ebenezer ("stone of help"), 1 Sam. 7:7-17. In spite of the fact that the return to the theocracy had brought great blessings and in spite of God's warning that establishing a monarchy would not be good, the people insisted, "We will have a king over us, that we also may be like all the nations," 1 Sam. 8:19-20.

God yielded to the people's request and selected an outstanding young farmer of the tribe of Benjamin ("there was not among the children of Israel a goodlier person than he," 1 Sam. 9:2) as the first king, and Samuel anointed him. The people happily chanted, "God save the king," 9—10. Saul started out well with a victory over the Ammonites, 11. Since this might lead the people to put too much trust in a king, Samuel urged both Saul and the people to put their trust in God and obey Him alone, 12. Saul failed in this when the Philistines came against Israel and even more when he was sent to destroy the Amalekites. Saul's disobedience resulted in God's and Samuel's sad rejection of him, 13—15.

God, however, was not at a loss as to what to do. He

sent Samuel to anoint Jesse's youngest son, David, as king and also arranged for David to soothe the spirit of Saul with music, 1 Sam. 16. Hereafter the Book of 1 Samuel tells the story of Saul, the king, and of David, the king-anointed, side by side until the end of the book, which also marks the end of Saul's life. We have the story of David and Goliath, 1 Sam. 17; of the great love of Jonathan, Saul's son, toward David and of Saul's bitter hatred toward David, 18—20.

With 1 Sam. 21 begins the sad account of David's flight from the hateful pursuit of King Saul, and this extends to 1 Sam. 26, where David has his final encounter with Saul. In this section we have the story of Samuel's death, 1 Sam. 25:1, and of the interesting meeting of Abigail, David's future wife, 25:2-43.

David felt he would be more safe if he gained the favor of the Philistines and actually joined their forces, 1 Sam. 27. Saul's frustration became ever more severe as the Philistines arose in battle again. He consulted a witch at Endor and requested to speak to Samuel even though he was dead. This experience gave Saul no hope nor help. The Philistines killed Saul's sons, also Jonathan, and Saul in utter despair committed suicide, 1 Sam. 28—31. What a dreadful end to the first king of Israel!

The Second Book of Samuel

This Second Book of Samuel could very well be described as the story of the reign of the second king of Israel, namely, David. It can be divided into four sections: the first seven and one half years of David's reign at Hebron, 2 Sam. 1—4 (cf. map); the change of capital from Hebron to Jerusalem and David's conquest of surrounding nations, 5—10; David's serious sin with Bathsheba and Absalom's rebellion with various evil results, 11—20; blessings and problems in the last years of David's reign, 21—24.

David demonstrated a noble attitude in dealing with

Saul's death, 2 Sam. 1. He is, however, kept from assuming full successorship to Saul, because Abner, the general of the army, promotes Saul's son, Ishbosheth, as king, 2. The third chapter begins with the words, "Now there was a long war between the house of Saul and the house of David." It came to an end when Abner turned against Ishbosheth and offered support to David, 3. David again conducted himself very nobly in all these events (death of Abner and of Ishbosheth) and won the loyalty of all the people, 4.

To establish his capital in a neutral place, David conquered the fortress of the Jebusites and built Jerusalem and brought the Ark of the Covenant there, 2 Sam. 5—6. David wanted to build a beautiful temple here but the Lord restrained him. Instead Nathan, the prophet, said to David, "The Lord telleth thee that He will make thee an house," 7:11. This is developed into a great Messianic prophecy. David responds with a psalm of gratitude, 7. The next three chapters recount one triumph of David after another over the various surrounding nations, 8—10.

Unfortunately, with great national success David fell into deep personal sin with Bathsheba, 2 Sam. 11. Nathan led David to sincere repentance, 12, but personal distresses followed for David: the little child died; serious family problems developed with Absalom, Amnon, and Tamar, David's children; 13; Absalom instituted a rebellion against David, drove him out of Jerusalem, and made war against him, 14—18. Absalom was killed and after much confusion, intrigue, and murder David was brought back as king in Jerusalem, 19—20.

Trouble was not at an end: a three-year famine and war against the Philistines followed, 2 Sam. 21. After God's deliverance David expressed gratitude in a beautiful psalm of praise, 22 (cf. Psalm 18). As David looked back upon his career, he recounted the help of many great men, 23. He made still another serious

mistake in trying to number the people, and God
responded with a plague, which was stopped when David
took the blame and was directed by God to buy a plot of
ground. David bought the threshingfloor of Araunah, the
Jebusite, where later the temple was built, 24. (Cf. also 1
Chron. 21—27.)

The First Book of Chronicles

We have here a recapitulation and an expansion of
much that was written in the Second Book of Samuel. In
the Hebrew Canon the First and Second Books of
Chronicles formed one book at the very end of the
Kethubim, the Sacred Writings. The title was Book of
Events or Acts or Annals. The Greek translation, the
Septuagint (LXX), divided it into two books with the
title: "Things Passed By" (*Paraleipomenon*). In the Latin
translation (the Vulgate), Jerome suggested the title by
which these books are known today: "Chronicles."

It is quite evident from the content that these
books were written very late and form companion
volumes to Ezra and Nehemiah. Many scholars consider
Ezra to be the writer, while others assume that it is the
composite work of a "school of writers" after the Exile.
Many different sources are mentioned as having been
used by these writers (cf. 1 Chron. 29:29; 2 Chron. 9:29;
12:15; 16:11; 20:34; 24:27; 26:22; 33:19; 35:25, 27). Whoever
wrote the book demonstrates that he had a good
knowledge of the history of God's people. Even though
the writer remains unknown, the canonicity of
Chronicles is established by the genealogies, cf. Matt. 1:1-
16 and Luke 3:23-38, and by such New Testament
references as Acts 7:47-52; Acts 17:24; Matt. 23:35; Luke
11:51.

Why do we discuss the First Book of Chronicles at
this point? Because, as indicated earlier, it recounts much
of what we are told in the Books of Samuel: 1 Chron. 1—9
present genealogies from Adam to the end of the Exile of

Judah; 1 Chron. 10 gives a brief account of Saul's reign; and 1 Chron. 11—29 present stories out of the life of David.

The book is written with a very distinct purpose and from a definitely religious point of view. It has been said that while the Books of Samuel and of Kings present matters as man sees them, the Books of Chronicles set them forth as God sees them. The focus is first on God's faithful dealing with His people, both in keeping promises and also in executing threats; and second on proper worship of God, with emphasis on the temple in Jerusalem. These foci must be taken into consideration when one reads these books and notices the selectivity of material presented; the almost total ignoring of the tribes of the north; some of the rhetorical forms; much greater emphasis on the favorable deeds of David than on his sins and weaknesses; and a generally strong moral and religious tone. It shows God's earnest efforts to keep His people true to Him.

The first genealogical table extends from Adam to Edom, 1 Chron. 1; the next from Israel (Jacob) to David, 2. Then are listed the descendants of David, 3; the descendants of Judah and Simeon, 4; the children of the tribes east of Jordan, Reuben, Gad, Manasseh, 5; the sons of Levi, 6; the line of Issachar, Benjamin, Naphtali, Manasseh, Ephraim, and Asher, 7; the posterity of Benjamin, 8; and the registration lists after the return from the Exile, 9.

To lead up to the life of David there is a very brief review of Saul's overthrow and death, 1 Chron. 10. Enthusiastically the writer turns attention to David and presents a long list of David's mighty men, 11 and 12. Then we read of David's attempt to bring the Ark of the Covenant to Jerusalem, 13; a victory over the Philistines, 14; the completion of bringing the Ark of the Covenant to Jerusalem with great joy, 15, and the singing of psalms, 16, cf. Pss. 96; 105:1-15; and 106:47, 48.

50

Even as in 2 Sam. 7, so here God responds to David's desire to build a temple with a distinct Messianic prophecy, 1 Chron. 17. David's successful conquest of neighboring nations is told in chapters 18—20. The accounts of David's sinful census and the resulting pestilence, halted graciously by God through an angel, supply the background for David's purchase of a plot for the temple, 21. Thereupon David made generous provision for the temple, encouraged Solomon to build, and set up a very elaborate ministry of the Levites for temple worship, 22—26. He also set up political officials, 27. Similar to Moses in Deuteronomy and Joshua in the last two chapters of the Book of Joshua, David delivers warm words of farewell to Solomon and to all the people, 28 and 29; and the concluding summary statement is made: "And he died in a good old age, full of days, riches, and honor; and Solomon his son reigned in his stead," 29:28.

The Book of Psalms

Before proceeding with the story of the third king of Israel, Solomon, the son of David, we shall take a brief look at the Book of Psalms, or the Psalter, because David, moved by the Holy Spirit, wrote more of these than any other writer, and he is the only writer of Psalms mentioned in the New Testament, Luke 20:42. Other writers of Psalms are Asaph, a Levite who was one of the leaders of David's choir in Jerusalem, who wrote 12; the sons of Korah, a celebrated family of singers (10), plus Ps. 88 by Heman, a son of Korah (1); Solomon (2); Moses (1), which is Ps. 90, the oldest of all; and Ethan, a temple musician (1). Some questions have been raised as to the implication of the preposition "to," e.g., "to David" in the superscription of a psalm, whether this expresses authorship or dedication. It certainly does indicate that David had much to do with the Psalms, "the hymnbook of the temple," and all that fits well with the great interest that David manifested in temple worship.

Whether some of the psalms are adaptations of Canaanite poems or of popular poetry of other nations cannot be definitely determined. Although parallels can be found in non-Biblical literature, the uniqueness of the 150 psalms in the Psalter is that all of these were inspired by the Holy Spirit. Comparing these inspired psalms with the poems and prayers of Mesopotamian and Egyptian origin reveals very distinct and striking differences.

The Psalms do not present a new theology but rather reflect the faith of God's people through the ages. In fact, the Jews found a reflection of the theme of the respective books of the Pentateuch in the five "books" into which the Psalms were divided. Each "book" closes with a similar doxology and a double Amen: Book I, Psalms 1—41 (like Genesis, concerning man and the Son of Man); Book II, Psalms 42—72 (like Exodus, concerning redemption); Book III, Psalms 73—89 (like Leviticus, concerning the sanctuary); Book IV, Psalms 90—106 (like Numbers, concerning life in this world as a wilderness); Book V, Psalms 107—150 (like Deuteronomy, concerning the Word of God). This parallel seems somewhat forced and fanciful, but it at least gives some reason for this grouping into five "books of psalms."

Some other forms of grouping are evident: with respect to writer, e.g., Pss. 3 ff.; 42 ff.; 73 ff.; with regard to outward relationship, e.g., Pss. 52 ff.; 120 ff. (psalms of degrees); with respect to similarity of contents, e.g., Pss. 95 ff.; 145 ff. This leads to the assumption that one individual, perhaps Ezra, as Jerome supposed, or Nehemiah, served as compiler. The authenticity, integrity, and canonicity of the Psalter have never been doubted either in the Jewish or in the Christian church.

Hebrew poetry is based on the concept of rhythmic expression of thought, consisting of corresponding parts or lines, as though the first is a statement and the next is an echo. These are known as parallelisms and may occur in two lines or stichs (distichs), Ps. 23:1; or three lines (tristichs), Ps. 6, 7; or four lines (tetrastichs), Ps. 5:10, etc. Monostichs (one line) are rare, Ps. 18:2. A parallelism may express a similar thought in every stich (synonymous), e.g., Ps. 2:4; 19:1; 118:1; or one stich may stand in contrast to the previous one (antithetic), e.g., Ps. 1:6; or one stich may complement or enlarge upon another (synthetic, emblematic, comparative), e.g., Ps. 19:8; 42:1. Some of the Psalms, e.g., 25; 34; 145; 119; 37, are acrostics, using the letters of the Hebrew alphabet in an artistic arrangement.

Another way to classify the Psalms is to consider the theme or chief emphasis of a respective psalm, e.g., comfort, Ps. 73; didactic, Ps. 1; penitential, Ps. 51; praise, Ps. 150; thanksgiving, Ps. 18; historical, Ps. 78; imprecatory, Ps. 35; and Messianic, Ps. 110. The latter two require special comment. Imprecatory psalms express curses upon the wicked and have been criticized as demonstrating a spirit contrary to the general Biblical emphasis of love and charity. The best explanation is to regard them as an expression, inspired by the Holy Spirit, of righteous moral indignation against evil. The Messianic psalms must be recognized and interpreted in the light of New Testament fulfillment and as such are among the most precious of all the psalms.

Some of the statements of Martin Luther in his Introduction to the Psalms, 1531 [1545], may serve well as a summary of this great book of the Old Testament: "The Book of Psalms is precious to us, first of all, on account of the references which it contains to the death and resurrection of Christ and the nature of His kingdom. One might call it a Little Bible or a beautiful summary of all that Scripture contains, a manual or handbook which the Holy Ghost Himself has caused to be written for those who cannot read all of the Bible. . . . Not only does the

Book of Psalms record deeds of the saints, but their words, how they spoke to God. They seem, indeed, to live as we hear them utter their prayers. . . . We can, as it were, look into their hearts, and observe their thoughts in the midst of all kinds of trouble. . . . Again, where do you find such expressions of joy as in the Psalms of Praise? As we look into the hearts of these sacred writers, we gaze into a beautiful garden, yes, into heaven itself, replete with flowers of praise and thanksgiving. . . . Thus we find in this precious Book a reflection of our own sorrows and joys, only stated much better than we can ever hope to do, and by making their thoughts our own, we dwell in the veritable communion of saints."

The First Book of Kings and The Second Book of Chronicles

In the original Hebrew manuscripts the two Books of Kings were one book. In the Greek translation, the Septuagint, they were divided into two books and designated as the Third and Fourth Book of Kings, since 1 and 2 Samuel were called the First and Second Book of Kings. A careful study of 1 and 2 Kings reveals that the theme and purpose and the language and style indicate them to be individual books, independent of 1 and 2 Samuel, with a different author. Who the author was is not determined. The Talmud regards Jeremiah as the author, and Biblical scholars have tended to agree because of various similarities of style and content, especially the literal agreement of 2 Kings 24:18—25:30 with Jeremiah 52. Various references are made to other sources: Acts of Solomon, Book of the Chronicles of the Kings of Judah, and Book of the Chronicles of the Kings of Israel. These New Testament references: Matt. 12:42 (1 Kings 10); Luke 4:25-27 (1 Kings 17); Acts 7:47 (1 Kings 6); Rom. 11:2-4 (1 Kings 19); James 5:17, 18 (1 Kings 17:1 and

18:41-45), corroborate the canonicity of this First Book of Kings.

A general outline of the book would be: the reign of Solomon, 1 Kings 1—11; the division of the kingdom, 12; the reign of Jeroboam to Ahaziah, son of Ahab, in the north, and the reign of Rehoboam to Jehoshaphat in the south, 13—22.

We shall at this point consider only the chapters relating the life and reign of Solomon in the first eleven chapters of 1 Kings and also utilize the first nine chapters of 2 Chronicles, as supplemental material. The first eight chapters of 2 Chronicles deal almost exclusively with Solomon's construction of the temple and establishing proper worship orders and services. 2 Chron. 9 tells of the Queen of Sheba's visit and her overwhelming astonishment at Solomon's wealth. We are told, "King Solomon passed all the kings of the earth in riches and wisdom," 9:22. The remaining chapters, 2 Chron. 10—36, tell the story of the kings ruling in the Kingdom of Judah, Rehoboam to Zedekiah. The last two verses of 2 Chron. 36 (22-23), briefly report that Cyrus, king of Persia, invited the Jews to return to Jerusalem to rebuild the temple. Thus 2 Chronicles begins with the building of the gorgeous temple of Solomon, leads us through almost four hundred years of Judah's history which resulted in the utter destruction of the Solomonic temple, and then ends with a brief reference to the next temple, which was completed in 516 B.C., seventy years after Solomon's temple was destroyed.

God wanted Solomon to be the third king over all of Israel but Adonijah, another son of David, tried in several different ways to usurp the throne, 1 Kings 1 and 2. God gave Solomon the opportunity to express a wish and Solomon requested wisdom, 2 Chron. 1. God was so pleased with this request that He said, "I have also given thee that which thou hast not asked, both riches and honor," 1 Kings 3:13. The gift of wisdom guided the young king to the "Solomonic decision" in the case of the two harlots, 1 Kings 3. The results of all three gifts, riches, honor, wisdom, in the life of Solomon are comprehensively presented in 1 Kings 4.

The next chapters describe in rather complete detail the building of the temple, thereby indicating its importance in the life of God's people. We are told of the alliance with King Hiram of Tyre for lumber for the temple, 1 Kings 5 and 2 Chron. 2. The construction is described in quite some detail, 1 Kings 6 and 7 and 2 Chron. 3 and 4. The account of the dedication of the temple gives a portrait of Solomon "in his finest hour," 1 Kings 8 and 2 Chron. 5—7.

Even though the next chapters, 1 Kings 9 and 10 and 2 Chron. 8 and 9, still relate positive events and even great praise in Solomon's life, one can already sense a spirit of secularism, which is then very forthrightly described in 1 Kings 11. Both accounts of Solomon's life end with these words, "And Solomon slept with his fathers, and was buried in the city of David, his father; and Rehoboam, his son, reigned in his stead," 1 Kings 11:43 and 2 Chron. 9:31.

The Book of Proverbs

The great charismatic gift to Solomon was wisdom which qualified him to produce 3,000 proverbs, 1 Kings 4:31, 32. There are 935 proverbs in this book, not all written by Solomon but all inspired by the Holy Spirit. They present wisdom as God's gift, precious in its own right. Wisdom is more than the opposite of ignorance; it is rather the opposite of foolishness and is the key to God's divine plan behind the whole creation, Prov. 30:3-5. Synonyms for "wisdom" in Proverbs are "understanding" (ability to comprehend); "knowledge" (ability to differentiate principles and premises); "learning" (process of development); "discernment" (distinguishing results and influences); "discretion" (exercising moderation); "prudence" (virtue of saying and doing the right thing at the right time), "fear of the Lord" (awe for majestic but loving God).

The great power and the real beauty of Proverbs are found in grasping the true meaning of "wisdom" by realizing that Jesus Christ, the Incarnate Word, John 1:1-18, is Personal Wisdom, Prov. 8 (cf. also Heb. 1:2; Col. 2:3), and the Fountain of all true wisdom. Thus this book gives us much more than moral direction. It pictures confident covenant living for the people of God. It is similar to Jesus' Sermon on the Mount and the Epistle of James in the New Testament.

The Hebrew word for "proverb" is "mashal," which may mean "maxim," but may also represent such broader literary devices as a "fable," "riddle," "satire," or "parable." They are not arranged in recognizable outline form but rather like pearls in a necklace. A general outline that has been suggested is the following: Solomon's praise of wisdom, Prov. 1—9; Solomon's proverbs on virtues and vices, Prov. 10:1—22:16; proverbs by various authors on many subjects, 22:17—24:34; Hezekiah's collection of Solomon's proverbs, 25—29; wisdom poems by Agur and Lemuel, 30—31. Another general outline: counsel for young men, Prov 1—10; counsel for all men, 11—20; counsel for kings and rulers, 21—31.

The canonicity of the Book of Proverbs was never questioned in the Jewish church and is corroborated by these New Testament references: Rom. 3:15 (Prov. 1:16); Rom. 12:20 (Prov. 25:21, 22); 1 Peter 4:8 (Prov. 10:12; 1 Peter 4:18 (Prov. 11:31); 2 Peter 2:22 (Prov. 26:11).

Martin Luther said of this Book of Proverbs: "It may rightly be called a book of good works; for Solomon here teaches the nature of a godly and useful life, so that every man aiming at godliness should make it his daily handbook or book of devotion and often read in it and compare with it his life." Two suggestions to help make the Book of Proverbs "a daily handbook or book of devotion" would be the following:

1. Discover these *pearls* of precious advice: to parents, Prov. 3:11-12; 13:24; 19:18; 22:6; 23:13, 14; 23:24, 25; 29:15; . . . to children, Prov. 1:7-9; 3:1-6; 3:11; 13:1; 15:32; 20:20; 23:26; 28:7; 30:17; . . . on poverty and riches, Prov. 10:15; 10:22; 14:20; 15:6; 15:16; 22:1, 2; 23:4, 5; 28:22; 30:7-9; . . . on stewardship, Prov. 3:9-10; 11:30; 19:17; 21:13; . . . on kindness of speech, Prov. 15:1; 25:11-12; . . . on cheerfulness, Prov. 17:22; . . . on humility, Prov. 15:33; 16:18; 18:12; 28:23; . . . on national integrity, Prov. 14:34;...against going security, Prov. 6:1-5;... on strife, Proverbs. 15:18; 17:14; 20:3; 26:21; 30:33; . . . on chastity, Prov. 5:1-12, 15-20.

2. Appreciate these meaningful *portraits:* of wisdom, Prov. 1:20-23; 3:13-18; 9:1-6; . . . of wisdom personified, Prov. 8:23-31; . . . of folly, Prov. 9:13-18; ...of a sadly misled youth, Prov. 7:6-23; . . . of a drunkard, Prov. 23:29-35; . . . of a lazy sluggard, Prov. 6:6-11; 26:13-16; . . . of a talebearer, Prov. 11:13; 17:9; 26:20; . . . of a slanderer, Prov. 4:24; 15:4; 15:28; 16:27; . . . of a liar, Prov. 6:16-19; 12:19; . . . of a virtuous woman, Prov. 31:10-31.

The Book of Ecclesiastes

Some scholars regard the Book of Ecclesiastes as a kind of challenge to the optimistic view of wisdom in the Book of Proverbs. These scholars feel that this type of bold challenge to orthodox Judaism might have been regarded as dangerously close to heresy and that, as a result, orthodox editors "touched up" Ecclesiastes to make it more palatable to orthodox taste. Other scholars seem to find strong Aramaic and even Greek influence in this book and conclude that this points to the postexilic age, considering 250 to 200 B.C. a likely date for its writing.

58

The title "Ecclesiastes" is a Greek translation of the Hebrew title "Koheleth" (Qoheleth) which may mean "one who assembles or collects" or "one who speaks in the assembly." The latter definition fits better to the Greek word *Ecclesiastes*, which means "a member of the assembly" or "a speaker in the assembly." This explains the title, "The Preacher," in the English versions. In the very first verse the "Preacher" is identified as "the son of David, king in Jerusalem," which, in our opinion, definitely points to Solomon as the author.

Much of the internal evidence indicates Solomonic authorship. Anyone who read 1 Kings 4:29-33 and there notes the wide educational interest and knowledge and the great wisdom of Solomon and then recognizes the keen perceptions and sharp insights in the Book of Ecclesiastes can readily agree that Solomon could logically be the author. The life of Solomon also fits so well to the picture of the tragic results of forsaking God and of seeking contentment in the transient "vanities" of the world presented in Ecclesiastes. The conclusion, "Fear God, and keep His commandments; for this is the whole duty of man," Eccl. 12:13, could very well be a fitting climax to the life of Solomon and his legacy of wisdom to the world after him. Because of the pessimistic and secularistic tone of the major portion of Ecclesiastes, it was one of three present canonical books (Esther and Song of Solomon, the other two) that the Jews questioned as to official inclusion in the canon. The Council of Jamnia, A.D. 90, officially recognized its canonicity. These New Testament passages seem to be allusions to parallels in Ecclesiastes: John 3:8 (Eccl. 11:5); Rom. 2:16 (Eccl. 12:14); 1 Tim. 1:5, 6 (Eccl. 12:13). Today the Jews read Ecclesiastes at the Feast of Tabernacles as a fitting reminder of the transiency of life (cf. Ps. 90).

It is difficult to develop a clear outline for the Book of Ecclesiastes. This very broad outline has been suggested: The things of this world are vain, Eccl. 1—6;

happiness can be found only in the fear of God, 7—12. Another outline is this: the theme "all is vanity," Eccl. 1:1-11; disappointing experiences with earthly pursuits, 1:12—2:26; worldly wisdom and its shortcomings, 3:1—11:8; the conclusion: God must be given the proper place in life, 11:9—12:14. Still another suggested outline: vanity of all earthly things stated in summary, Eccl. 1:1-11; evidence of the vanity of all earthly things from the writer's personal experience and general observation, 1:12—6:12; lessons to be learned from these experiences and observations, 7:1—12:8; the final conclusion, 12:9-14.

In Eccl. 12:11 we read of "goads" (questions which stimulate thought and action) and of "nails" (things to hold on to in facing life). This can form still another helpful outline: *Goad:* striving after earthly things is frustrating (Eccl. 1:1-2, 23); *Nail:* accept the good from God's hand and be content (2:24—3:15); *Goad:* men and animals die; where is there any difference? (3:16—4:16); *Nail:* go to God's house and listen to His Word (5:1-20); *Goad:* who even knows what's good for man? (6:1-12); *Nail:* wisdom is the good thing (7:1-29); *Goad:* who has wisdom? (8:1); *Nail:* he has wisdom who discerns time and judgment and walks in the fear of the Lord (8:2—12:14).

The three most striking terms in Ecclesiastes are "vanity": inability of mere earthly things to satisfy the desires of life; "nothing new": life is a weary course of cycles; "appointed time": each time in life is a purposeful opportunity provided by God. Martin Luther gives a good summary: "This book teaches primarily that everyone is to serve faithfully in his vocation, live in the fear of God, and commend all else, no matter what may happen, to God."

The Song of Solomon

This is a much disputed book, both as to origin and authorship and also as to interpretation and purpose.

The title in the very first verse: "The Song of Songs, which is Solomon's," seems definitely to point to Solomon as the writer. There are also other references to Solomon (1:5; 3:7-11; 8:11-12). In 1 Kings 4:32 we are told that Solomon's "songs were a thousand and five." It is assumed that the accepted Solomonic authorship led the Jews to affirm the canonicity of the Song of Solomon, even though many questioned its inclusion in the canon. Today the Jews read it at the Passover Festival as an expression of God's love for Israel, demonstrated particularly in the deliverance from Egypt.

Among the many different views which scholars have expressed concerning this Song of Songs are the following: a group of 24 or more wedding songs; a drama narrating the triumph of true love over social rank; a poetically idealized presentation of a love affair Solomon had with a Shulamite maid; a secular bridal hymn composed for Solomon; an anthology of lyrics adopting the mores and clichés of love prevalent in ancient Semitic society; the story of a "triangle" of a love affair involving Solomon, a young maiden, and a shepherd; or a reflection of the fertility cults in Canaan.

At the Council of Jamnia (A.D. 90), the Jewish Rabbi Akiba is credited with the dramatic statement, "No day outweighed in glory the one on which Israel received the Song of Solomon." Rabbi Akiba accepted the Jewish interpretation of the Song of Solomon as an allegorical presentation of God's love for Israel. This is still a popular Jewish interpretation: allegory of God's love expressed at Sinai, Song of Solomon 1 and 2; in the period of the Judges, 3:1-5; in the golden era of Israel's history, 3:6-8, 14.

Most Christian scholars have interpreted the Song of Solomon allegorically as a picture of Christ's love for the church. This seems warranted since other Scripture references draw similar pictures: Psalm 45; Hos. 2:19, 20; Matt. 9:15; John 3:29; and especially Eph. 5:25-29. Those who accept the allegorical interpretation and read the book carefully to discern who is speaking or singing (the bridegroom, the bride, or the daughters of Jerusalem) can be deeply strengthened in their faith that "Christ loved the church and gave Himself up for her" (Eph. 5:25).

This outline in the light of allegorical interpretation has been suggested for the book: The lovers sing of their love for one another (church reunited with Christ after a separation), Song of Solomon 1:2—2:7; groom bids bride to come with him and the bride responds positively (church is led to active service by Christ), 2:8-17; bride loses her groom but later finds him again and the wedding takes place (church often loses close relationship to Christ but is drawn back by His love) 3:1—5:1; the bride scorns the groom's love but later changes her mind and reconciliation results (church becomes careless but repents and Christ forgives), 5:2—6:9; mutual praise of bride and groom (church and Christ knit in mutual love and service), 6:10—8:4; pledge of eternal loyalty (the church forever at home with Christ) 8:5-14.

Whether one interprets the Song of Solomon literally as an exalted description of human love (and it cannot be less than that since it is the inspired Word of God), or as an allegorical portrayal of God's love for Israel or Christ's love for the church, the Christian will recognize that all human love can never approach the depth and height and breadth of the love of Christ, Eph. 3:18, 19, which runs as a golden thread through all of Scripture and gives the key to its proper interpretation.

4

The Divided Kingdom to Fall of Samaria, 722 B.C.

1 Kings 12—2 Kings 17—2 Chronicles 10—30

The Books of Kings and Chronicles have been introduced previously and will henceforth be referred to as historical background for placement and analysis of the Books of the Prophets which will be presented, as much as possible, in chronological sequence rather than in the order in which they are arranged in modern versions of the Bible.

It would be difficult to appreciate the significance of the Books of the Prophets if one did not understand the cataclysmic and catastrophic changes that occurred among God's people as they moved from the theocracy (God rules directly) through the hierocracy (priest rules) to the monarchy (one king rules), and then to a divided kingdom (Northern [Israel] and Southern [Judah]). To many of the children of Israel the establishment of a monarchy seemed to have been not only the transition they needed to become "like the nations" but had also catapulted their little nation into a position of recognition and prominence in the world. The period of David's and Solomon's reign is often referred to as "the golden age of Israel."

Many of the surrounding nations and tribes had been conquered. Especially under Solomon, world trade had been developed and great wealth flowed into Jerusalem. People all over the Fertile Crescent and beyond spoke with admiration about the great wisdom of Solomon. Rulers, including even Pharaoh Shishak of Egypt, were proud to have their daughters join the harem of Solomon, especially since Solomon permitted them to bring their form of idol worship with them. He even joined them in their idolatry.

But we read in 1 Kings 11:9: "The Lord was angry with Solomon, because his heart had turned away from the Lord, the God of Israel." God announced His displeasure to Solomon and told him that He would "tear the kingdom" from Solomon and from his son but allow him and his descendants to rule over one tribe "for the sake of David, My servant, and for the sake of Jerusalem which I have chosen," 1 Kings 11:11-13. The rest of the eleventh chapter of 1 Kings tells not only of the Edomites and Syrians rising up against Solomon but also of the insurrection of one of his own labor officers, Jeroboam of the tribe of Ephraim, who fled to Egypt until Solomon had died, 1 Kings 11:26-43.

Rehoboam, Solomon's son, was aware of some of the restlessness and resentment among the people but boldly asserted his authority as king over all of Israel. Jeroboam had received God's message through the Prophet Ahijah that he would rule over ten tribes, so upon hearing of Solomon's death he returned from Egypt and opposed Rehoboam, 1 Kings 12. Because the people had already become confused and dulled in their monotheistic loyalty to Jahweh, the true God of the covenant, through the syncretistic practices of Solomon, Jeroboam was able to set up "places of worship" in Bethel and in Dan to substitute for worship in Jerusalem without serious negative reaction from the people.

Thus God's people were divided, never to be brought together as one people again. Jealousy and animosity toward the tribe of Judah which had smoldered for quite some time already (cf. 2 Sam. 2:12-17; 19:41-43; 20:1-2) broke into open warfare under Kings Rehoboam, Abijah, and Asa of the Southern Kingdom (Judah) and Kings Jeroboam, Nadab, Baasha, Elah, Zimri, and Omri of the Northern Kingdom (The Ten Tribes), 1 Kings 12—16; 2 Chron. 10—16.

As one reads of the conduct of these kings, one can readily understand and appreciate God's future dealing with His people not through these kings, who were not chosen by Him and were leading the people "like the nations," but through prophets that He would call and to whom and through whom He would reveal His Word to His people.

The most commom Hebrew word for "prophet" is *nabi,* the plural *nebi'im.* The English word "prophet" is derived from a combination of two Greek words: *pro* (which can have a local designation "in front of" and a temporal meaning "before") and *phemi,* participle *phetes* (which means "I speak," participle "spoken"). Accordingly, a "prophet" is both a "forthteller" ("speaking in front of people") and a "foreteller" ("announcing a future happening"). The prophets of Israel served both functions, preaching God's message to His people, and telling God's people messages about the future that only God could know.

God imparted His message to the prophets in various ways: through direct inspiration, through dreams, and through ecstatic visions. The prophets knew that they were proclaiming God's message; therefore, hundreds of times they prefaced their message with the words, "Thus saith the Lord." In this way they differed significantly from the "seers" and "diviners" of the heathen tribes and also from "false prophets" who tried to pose as prophets of God even among God's people. On the occasion when God gave the Messianic prophecy through Moses that He would send a prophet like Moses,

Deut. 18:15, God also gave His people criteria by which to identify a false prophet, Deut. 18:20-22.

The prophets that are best known today are the "writing" or "literary" prophets. These men were "moved by the Holy Spirit" (2 Peter 1:21) to write down some of their messages and prophecies, and their names are thus mentioned more often. It cannot be determined in every instance whether the prophet did the writing or whether others wrote what the prophet preached. Prophets whose names are not associated with the writing of prophetical material are called "oral" prophets. Many of these receive only brief reference in Scripture, e.g., Shemaiah, Ahijah, Azariah, Hanani, Jehu, Jehaziel, Eliezer, Micaiah, also one prophetess, Huldah; but two oral prophets are given much attention in the Books of the Kings. They are Elijah and Elisha. The activity of Elijah is presented in 1 Kings 17—21 and 2 Kings 1 and 2; and the ministry of Elisha is related in 2 Kings 2—13. There are definite similarities in the prophetic careers of these two men: both parted the Jordan (2 Kings 2:8 and 2:14); both brought forth water miraculously (1 Kings 18:41-45 and 2 Kings 3:9-20); both provided food for widows (1 Kings 17:10-16 and 2 Kings 4:1-7); both raised a dead child to life (1 Kings 17:17-24 and 2 Kings 4:18-35); both announced judgment to kings (1 Kings 21:19-22 and 2 Kings 8:7-10); and both helped people outside of Israel (1 Kings 17:9-16 and 2 Kings 5:1-15). Yet the ministry of each had many unique features. Elijah seems to have been more dramatic and Elisha more pastoral, but both were fearless dedicated spokesmen and servants of God. Their names (Elijah: "Jahweh is my God," and Elisha: "My God has saved"), as in the case of many of the prophets, give a clue to their prophetic activity and message. The ministry of Elijah was primarily devoted to the time that King Ahab ruled over the north (Israel), 1 Kings 18—22, and King Jehoshaphat ruled in the south (Judah), 2 Chron. 17—20. Elisha served for a longer period while the following kings were ruling in the north (Israel): Ahaziah, Jehoram, Jehu, Jehoahaz, and Jehoash, 2 Kings 1—14; and these kings in the south (Judah): Jehoram, Ahaziah, Athaliah (the queen who usurped the throne), and Joash, 2 Chron. 21—24. It is in this period of time, while King Jehoram was ruling in Judah, that we place the book of the first writing or literary prophet, Obadiah. He is one of the twelve "minor prophets." This distinction of "minor" and "major" does not refer to the authenticity or importance of their message but rather to the extent or amount of their prophetic messages included in the Scripture. In other words, the "major" prophetical books are longer than those of the "minor" prophets.

The Book of Obadiah

Twelve people in the Old Testament carry the name "Obadiah" ("servant of Jahweh") and since no biographical information is given about this prophet, his identity remains undetermined. Some scholars believe he could be "Obadiah, the prince" who was sent out along with other princes by King Jehoshaphat, 2 Chron. 17:7-9, to teach the people of Judah. He could thus have participated in the battle which Jehoram, the son of Jehoshaphat, fought to quell the revolt of Edom, 2 Chron. 21:8-10. That would have given him eyewitness experience with Edom and would have equipped him well to write this inspired "vision" of judgment against Edom.

This leads many to regard Obadiah as the first of the writing prophets and to assume that other prophets quoted his writing: e.g., Jer. 49:7-22 (Obad. 1—6); Joel 2:32; 3:3; 3:19 (Obad. 17); Amos 9:2, 12, 14 (Obad. 4, 19, 20). Many others, however, contend that Obadiah was a contemporary of Jeremiah and quotes from the writings of Jeremiah, Joel, and Amos rather than they from him. There are plausible arguments for either viewpoint.

This book is the shortest in the entire Old Testament. The Jews referred to it as "the mustard seed"—both because of its brevity and also because of its bitterness in denouncing the Edomites, the descendants of Esau, the brother of Jacob. Esau settled south of the Dead Sea, and the Edomites became a proud warring nation, often going out on raiding expeditions and then retreating to Mt. Seir, a range of precipitous red sandstone heights quite inaccessible to any invaders. Bitter animosity and hatred existed toward the Jews, demonstrated already in refusing to let the children of Israel pass through their land in the wilderness journey, Num. 20:14-21, and increasing as time went on.

The great lessons taught by Obadiah are the certain punishment and doom of the proud and rebellious (Edom) and the deliverance of the meek and the humble (Jacob).

In clear unmistakable terms God points out that none of the things in which Edom has proudly placed its confidence (living in the clefts of the rock, strong allies, wise men, mighty men) will preserve it from the judgment He will send, Obad. 1-9. To justify His judgment God enumerates the sins of Edom: violence, v. 10; hostility, v. 11; rejoicing over Israel's calamity, v. 12; boasting, v. 12b; plundering Israel, v. 13; treatment of refugees, v. 14. "The day of the Lord" is near for Edom and all nations like her, vs. 15, 16; "but in Mt. Zion there shall be those that escape," v. 17. Thus Obadiah ends his message on a note of comfort and hope. While Edom and all wicked nations shall be utterly destroyed, God's people shall be safe and blessed "and the kingdom shall be the Lord's," vs. 18-21.

The Book of Joel

The prophet Joel ("Jahweh is God") gives no more biographical information about himself than that he was "the son of Pethuel." It seems that he lived in Jerusalem and directed his message primarily to Judah in the early period of the reign of King Joash, although many Bible students hold that he lived in the sixth or even the fifth century before the birth of Christ. Some of the arguments in favor of placing Joel at the time of King Joash are these: (1) Joel wrote after the victory of Jehoshaphat over the Moabites and Ammonites, cf. Joel 3:2 and 2 Chron. 20:1-26; (2) Joel mentions the Phoenicians, Philistines, Egyptians, and Edomites as enemies of Judah, Joel 3:4, 19; (3) Assyria, Babylonia, and Persia, later enemies of God's people, are not mentioned; (4) good worship practices seem to prevail, as in the early days of the reign of Joash, Joel 1:9, 13, 14, 16; 2:1, 14-17; 2 Chron. 23:16, 17; and 2 Chron. 24:14; (5) there is evidence of close relation to Obadiah, cf. Joel 2:32—Obad. 17; Joel 3:3—Obad. 11; Joel 3:19—Obad. 10; and to Amos, cf. Joel 3:16—Amos 1:2; Joel 3:18—Amos 9:13. The canonicity of the Book of Joel is affirmed by Acts 2:16-21 (Joel 2:28-32) and by Rom. 10:13 (Joel 2:32).

The description of the plague is vivid and graphic: old men can not recall a similar one, Joel 1:2; different stages of locusts take their toll, 1:4; locusts are pictured as fierce enemies, 1:6-8; 2:4-9; the devastating results are horrible, Joel 1:9-20; 2:1-3; 2:10-11. (An account of a very similar locust plague in modern times in that area is found in *The National Geographic Magazine*, Vol. XXVIII, p. 511 ff.)

Joel's call to repentance is, "Rend your hearts and not your garments, return to the Lord, your God," Joel 2:13. This catastrophe was to induce them to institute a series of worship services and offerings to demonstrate their sorrow over their sins, Joel 2:14-17.

The people responded. "Then the Lord became jealous for His land and had pity on His people," Joel 2:18. God gives them four great promises: (1) instead of drought and devastation there will be bounteous crops, Joel 2:19-27; (2) God will marvelously bless them with

His Holy Spirit, Joel 2:28-32 (cf. Acts 2:16-210; (3) nations that have afflicted Judah will be punished, Joel 3:1-15; (4) God's covenant people in the future, even into eternity, will be blessed, Joel 3:16.21.

The Book of Jonah

In 2 Kings 14:25 reference is made to the Prophet Jonah in these words, "He (Jeroboam II) restored the border of Israel from the entrance of Hamath as far as the Sea of the Arabah, according to the Word of the Lord, the God of Israel, which He spoke by His servant, Jonah, the son of Amittai, the prophet, who was from Gathhepher." Thus Jonah's political mission as a prophet was to tell Jeroboam II that God would grant Israel military success under his leadership. The reign of Jeroboam II marked the highpoint of Israel's (the Northern Kingdom) history in military conquest and in prosperity, and in agriculture and business. A picture of these prosperous times in Israel is also presented in references in the Book of Hosea and the Book of Amos, supported by excavations at Megiddo and Samaria.

But, God had another mission for Jonah which is recounted in the book which bears his name. This was the mission of preaching repentance to Nineveh, the capital of Assyria. Modern critical scholarship questions whether this was the same man as the prophet sent to Jeroboam II. The threefold identity of the man in Jonah 1:1 with the man in 2 Kings 14:25 (name, name of father, and office of a prophet) led the ancient Jewish and the early Christian church to regard him as the same individual. However, since the Book of Jonah is written in the third person, different from other prophetical books, many modern scholars have assumed that it was not written by the historical Jonah (2 Kings 14:25) but composed much later. Many hold that it is not a historical account at all but rather a parable to reveal

God's displeasure over exclusivistic pride and false superiority.

Because of unusual events related in the Book of Jonah (swallowed by a great fish and spewed out alive, the repentance en masse of Nineveh, the gourd and the worm), Bible students have expressed many different views concerning its literary genre. A few of these are the following: a blend of prose and poetry with no historical significance; a parable told in historical style to teach the universality of God's mercy; a type of high class Jewish humor; a dream Jonah had without an actual experience of the events related; a legend about a mythical prophet who brought messages of peace, symbolized by the name "Jonah" which means "dove"; a Fertile Crescent fable with a fish motif depicting the hostility of the sea; a dramatic portrayal of man's reversal of fortune illustrated by Jonah's encounter with the fish; a popular myth to remind the Jews, especially during the reformations of Ezra and Nehemiah, that Jahweh is ready to be the God of all and that they should therefore not despise other nations and people.

Although some of the miracles seem quite unusual and some difficulties of interpretation remain, the traditional view, which regards this book as actual history, is the most compatible with the New Testament references in Matt. 12:39-41 and 16:4 (the sign of Jonah in the belly of the fish) and Luke 11:29, 30, 32 (the repentance of Nineveh). Many people who have a casual acquaintance with the Book of Jonah express primary interest in the great fish or in Jonah or in Nineveh but fail to appreciate the central emphasis on the all-embracing love and the powerful providence of God. God, not Jonah, is the most prominent character in this book.

A brief outline of the book is: First Call of Jonah, Jonah 1:1-2; Jonah's Response and the Results, 1, 3—2:10; Second Call of Jonah, 3:1-2; Jonah's Response and the Results, 3:3—4:11. A somewhat more detailed outline is this: God calls Jonah to preach repentance to Nineveh but Jonah responds by boarding a ship to Tarshish, 1:1-4. God sends a storm and Jonah is cast into the sea, 1:5-15. God arranges for a great fish to swallow Jonah, 1:16-17. Jonah prays and God delivers him, 2:1-10. Now Jonah obeys God's call and preaches to Nineveh, 3:1-4. Nineveh repents and God spares it from destruction, 3:5-10. Jonah expresses his disappointment that the city is spared, 4:1-4. God rebukes Jonah for his lack of compassion by the illustration of the quick growth and equally quick destruction of a gourd, 4:5-11.

The Book of Amos

The historical background for the Book of Amos is sketched in 2 Kings 14:1 to 2 Kings 15:7 and in 2 Chron. 25 and 26. These were the years when Jeroboam II ruled in Israel, and Amaziah and Uzziah (Azariah) ruled in Judah. It was an era of great prosperity in both kingdoms (the northern and the southern). In the Northern Kingdom Jeroboam II conquered Damascus, the capital of Syria, and even Hamath, a city of the Hittites, about 200 miles north of Damascus. In the Southern Kingdom Uzziah subdued the Philistines and Arabians; made vassals of the Amorites; built strong outposts in the deserts of Judah; fortified Jerusalem with towers; had a standing army of 307,500 men fully equipped with the most modern weapons of warfare; and maintained outward peace with Jeroboam II. Uzziah also fostered agricultural development, the planting of orchards and vineyards, and the cultivation of farms and gardens.

From all outward appearance, these days of peace and prosperity were similar to the golden era of the United Kingdom under David and Solomon. But the social conditions were appalling. Both kingdoms, but particularly the Northern Kingdom, were decaying internally because of moral, political, social, and

72

spiritual evils: oppression of the poor; corruption of justice and of politics; concentration of wealth in the hands of few; overindulgence in luxuries; high prevalence of gluttony, drunkenness, immorality, greed, and unconcern for others; and rampant idolatry, although some weak and anemic worship of Jahweh, the God of the covenant, still existed.

God called a farmer from Tekoa, a small village about twelve miles south of Jerusalem, to be His witness against these evils. His name was Amos, which is derived from the verb "to bear" or "to place a load upon." Amos refers to himself as "a herdsman, and a dresser of sycamore trees," Amos 7:14. A herdsman was more a breeder of sheep than a shepherd, but Amos says he "followed the flock," 7:15. As a dresser or cultivator of sycamore fruit (a type of mulberry fig), Amos punctured the fruit so that insects which formed on the inside were released and the fruit was made edible. Amos seems, therefore, to have been a rather ordinary farmer, but his writing reveals keen perception and an astounding knowledge of history, politics, international relations, geography, sociology, astronomy, and theology. Inspired by the Holy Spirit, Amos scathingly denounced the prevailing sins and proclaimed God's judgment with courage and power.

Even though Amos lived in Judah, God called him to be a prophet in Israel, primarily in the area of Bethel, one of the centers of idol worship for the tribes of the north. Amos' preaching irritated Amaziah, the priest of Bethel, who complained to King Jeroboam II, but Amos stood firm on the basis of his divine call and continued to preach. Later he returned to Judah and wrote this book, inspired by the Holy Spirit, as a summary of his entire prophetic activity. The canonicity has never been in doubt and is affirmed by these New Testament references: Acts 7:42 (Amos 5:25) and Acts 15:15-17 (Amos 9:11, 12).

Two major divisions are plainly evident: Amos 1—6:

Judgment upon surrounding nations and Judah and then upon Israel; Amos 7—9: Visions of the future of Israel. In announcing the judgment, Amos usually singles out one outstanding sin but adds that there are three and four and even more. These announcements of judgment are arranged in strophic members: Amos 1:3-5. Syria (cruelty); 1:6-8, Philistia (slave-trade); 1:9-10, Phoenicia (truce-breaking); 1:11-12, Edom (irreconcilability); 1:13-14; Ammon (mad aggression); 2:1-3, Moab (vengeance); 2:4-5, Judah (idolatry); 2:6-16, Israel (pride).

Three prophetic orations follow, each beginning with a call to listen, "Hear this word," Amos 3:1; 4:1; 5:1. In the first oration Amos reasons with the people to recognize the imminence of the judgment, Amos 3:1-15. In the second he chastises the arrogant women ("cows of Bashan," 4:1) and holds them responsible for many of the sins among Israel, 4:1-13. In the third he expresses the grief of God over their sin, 5:1-25; he also appeals specifically to them, "Seek the Lord and live," 5:4, 6, 14. The people of Israel are so secure and self-confident in their prosperity that Amos cries out to them, "Woe to those who are at ease in Zion," 6:1-14.

In the second major section Amos prophesies the coming judgment of Israel in five visions: the devouring locust, Amos 7:1-3; the consuming fire, 7:4-6; the searching plumbline, 7:7-11; (a brief historical interlude, 7:12-17); the basket of summer fruit, 8:1-14; and the Lord at the altar, 9:1-10.

After unloading the burden of judgment, Amos closes the prophecy with a thrilling message of hope and of blessing for God's people. In Acts 15:16, 17, the apostle Paul shows that Amos was prophesying about the inclusion of the Gentiles in the kingdom of God, Amos 9:11-15.

The literary style of Amos is stimulating because he employs expressive references to nature and rural life to present a forthright spiritual message: overloading a wagon (sinners straining God's mercy), Amos 2:13; roaring of a lion (pressure of obligation), 3:8; shepherd recovering part of a sheep (the remnant of Israel), 3:12; a brand plucked out of a fire (narrow escape of Israel), 4:11; the mountains and the wind (God's power), 4:13; the constellations (God's majesty), 5:8; luscious ripe summer fruit (imminence of decay), 8:1. Many of the statements in the Book of Amos (e.g., 3:3; 3:6; 4:12; 6:1; 7:14) are frequently quoted in various contexts today. Bible students agree that "the Book of Amos has a remarkable relevance to modern times."

The Book of Hosea

When Amos was nearing the end of his prophetic ministry, God called Hosea to prophesy to the Northern Kingdom. His name means "Jahweh has saved." Hosea has been called "the impassioned prophet of God's love to Israel" because his marriage to Gomer, a harlot, symbolized the depth of divine love for unlovely mankind. He is also known as "the deathbed prophet of Israel," because he is the last of the prophets before Israel's annihilation by Assyria. He is, as it were, standing at the deathbed of Israel with a final fervent exhortation and plea to return to God, "Come, let us return to the Lord; for He has torn, that He may heal us," Hos. 6:1. Hosea uses the word "return" fifteen times in this book.

No further personal information about Hosea's ancestry is given, other than that he was the son of Beeri, who is unidentified. The time period is, however, clearly set by naming Jeroboam II as the king of Israel and Uzziah, Jotham, Ahaz, and Hezekiah as kings of Judah. Hosea's early prophecies, Hos. 1—3, were delivered during the last days of Jeroboam's reign, and the latter prophecies, Hos. 4—14, during the turbulent years that followed Jeroboam's death when the last six kings of

Israel, Zachariah, Shallum, Menahem, Pekahiah, Pekah, and Hoshea followed one another in rapid succession. Prosperity and security were replaced by confusion, demoralization, and anxiety because of international developments, 2 Kings 15:8—17:41.

Shortly after the death of Jeroboam II, Tiglath-pileser III, referred to as Pul in the Scriptures, became ruler of Assyria and started an aggressive conquest to gain control of the Fertile Crescent. He conquered Babylonia and then marched westward to take Syria and Palestine. His military policy was to take the most able citizens of conquered nations into exile and resettle the land with foreign colonists. This caused consternation and terror among Israel and Judah. Domestic turmoil also troubled Israel: Zachariah ruled only six months and was murdered by Shallum, who was killed by Menahem after ruling only one month. Menahem ruled for ten years and died a natural death, but his son and successor, Pekahiah, was killed after ruling only two years. His successor, Pekah, the former army commander, was killed by Hoshea, who became the last king of Israel. During all this turmoil the prophet Hosea was the voice of the Lord. Late in his life Hosea by the inspiration of the Holy Spirit wrote his oral prophecies in condensed form in this book. No doubt has ever been expressed about the authenticity or canonicity of this book. These New Testament references serve as corroborating evidence: Rom. 9:25, 26 and 1 Peter 2:10 (Hos. 1:10—2:1, 23); Matt. 2:15 (Hos. 11:1); Matt. 9:13 and Matt. 12:7 (Hos. 6:6); Luke 23:30 and Rev. 6:16 (Hos. 10:8); 1 Cor. 15:55, 57 (Hos. 13:14).

This is a brief outline of the book: Hosea's relation to his harlot wife, Gomer, typifies God's love for His people requited by their idolatrous (adulterous) behavior; Hos. 1:2—3:5. This reaction demands punishment, 4:1—5:15. God pleads for a return of His people and gives a promise, 6:1-3. Israel reacts negatively and in extended discourses God explains why He must punish, 6:4—13:8. Israel has brought about its own doom, 13:9-13. However, a ransom is paid and Israel is forgiven and gracious blessings abound, 13:14—14:9.

It must have been very difficult for Hosea to obey the Lord's command to marry a harlot, Hos. 1:2, but he did it. He married Gomer and three children were born and were given meaningful names: Jezreel ("God scatters"), 1:4; Lo-Ruhamah ("no mercy" or "not pitied"), 1:8; Lo-Ammi ("not my people"), 1:9. Gomer ran away and left Hosea with his two young sons and a daughter. Hosea continued to love her and tried to win her back. All this is a beautiful symbol of God's love for Israel and for all His people. Hosea uses various symbolic expressions to picture the rebellious attitude of Israel: an adulterous wife, Hos. 3:1; a wine-inflamed drunkard, 4:11; a stubborn heifer, 4:16; troops of robbers, 6:9; adulterers, 7:4; hot as an oven, 7:7; a half-baked cake, 7:8; a silly dove, 7:11; a treacherous bow, 7:16; a useless vessel, 8:8; a wild ass, 8:9.

Against such a background of unfaithfulness and rebellion, the undeserved and unending love of God appears all the brighter and more precious. It is expressed in the simple words of Hos. 11:1: "When Israel was a child I loved him, and out of Egypt I called My son." No one will ever be able to explain why God selected Israel out of all the people of the world in any other way than to attribute it to God's ineffable love. In Matt. 2:15 this text (Hos. 11:1) is demonstrated to be a Messianic prophecy referring to Christ's return from Egypt. In Christ God gives men the strongest and greatest revelation of His never-ending love.

The Book of Isaiah

Israel was conquered by Assyria in 722 B.C. By that time Isaiah had already been a prophet in Jerusalem, in the Kingdom of Judah, for twenty years. He was called a prophet in 742 B.C., "the year that King Uzziah died," Is. 6:1. Not much biographical information is available. He was the son of Amoz (no relation to Amos, the prophet). There is a Jewish tradition that he was of royal descent, a cousin of King Uzziah. He states that he prophesied during the reign of Uzziah, Jotham, Ahaz, and Hezekiah, Is. 1:1. During the last years of his reign Uzziah was ill with leprosy and his son, Jotham, was coregent with him, 2 Chron. 26:19-21. The first five chapters of the Book of Isaiah give a picture of prevailing social conditions during the reign of Uzziah and Jotham. They can be summed up well in the three words: formalism, materialism, and vanity, Is. 1—3; for which God announced His judgment upon Judah, 4—5. The fifth chapter closes with the ominous words, "And if one look to the land, behold, darkness and distress; and the light is darkened by its clouds," 5:30.

In strong contrast the divine call to Isaiah in the next chapter presents God in His majesty but also in His gracious love to cleanse the unclean and to send them out to be His messengers, Is. 6:1-13. While Jotham was king, Pekah, the king of Israel, formed an alliance with Rezin, the king of Syria, to withstand Tiglath-pileser, ruler of Assyria, and to fight together against Judah. Ahaz succeeded Jotham, his father, as king and was confronted by this Syro-Israelite alliance. "His heart and the heart of his people shook as the trees of the harvest shake before the wind," 7:2.

God told Isaiah to meet Ahaz at the water pool and to take his son with him. Isaiah's son had the meaningful name Shearjashub ("a remnant shall return"), Is. 7:3. Isaiah told Ahaz, "Be quiet, do not fear," 7:4, and predicted that Rezin and Pekah would do him no harm. He even offered Ahaz the opportunity to ask for a substantiating sign, but Ahaz declined, 7:10-12. Isaiah nonetheless announced the sign of the birth of a child that would be called Immanuel ("God with us"), 7:14.

78

This passage is interpreted by some as a successive prophecy, first fulfilled at the time of Ahaz by a young woman, possibly his own wife, in the birth of their son, Hezekiah. Others understand this verse as a direct prophecy referring to the Virgin Mary (Hebrew, *almah*, "virgin" or "young woman") and the birth of Jesus. In Matt. 1:23, the Holy Spirit, who is the Author of both the Old Testament and the New Testament account, records the fulfillment of His prophetic Word in the virgin birth of Christ, Immanuel. Isaiah prophesied that this child would demonstrate that God is with His people and will deliver them, Is. 7:13-25. In the next chapter the other son of Isaiah is introduced. He had the expressive name Mahershalalhashbaz ("make speed to the spoil—hasten to the prey"), 8:1. Isaiah prophesied that before this son could talk both Syria and Israel would be conquered, but Ahaz still refused to listen and to trust in God, 8:2-22. In disbelief he even made an alliance with Tiglath-pileser and obtained blueprints for an Assyrian altar to be built in Jerusalem, 2 Kings 16:7-20 and 2 Chron. 28:16-27.

Isaiah pointed beyond the days of Ahaz to the mighty Messiah whom God would send, Is. 9:1-7, but threatened judgment if Judah would reject Him and His promises, 9:8-21. He announced that Assyria would be destroyed, 10:1-34, and then painted an inspiring picture of the kingdom of the Messiah, 11:1—12:6.

In the second major section of the first part of the book, Isaiah announces God's message of judgment against the wicked nations that oppose those who trust in Jahweh: Babylon, Is. 13:1—14:27; Philistia, 14:28-32; Moab, 15:1—16:13; Syria, 17:1-3; Israel 17:4-11; Assyria, 17:12-14; Egypt and Ethiopia, 18:1—20:6; Babylon, 21:1-10; Edom, 21:11-12; Arabia, 21:13-16; Jerusalem, Valley of Visions, 22:1-25; Tyre, 23:1-18. This is followed by a "great symphony in four movements": God's dreadful judgments, 24:1-23; the revelation of Jahweh, 25:1-12; a hymn encouraging confidence in God, 26:1-21; and a song of praise declaring that God takes care of His vineyard, 27:1-13.

In the next eight chapters (Is. 28—35) Isaiah records a series of prophecies and proclamations concerning the relation of Judah to Assyria under King Hezekiah. The key statement is found in Is. 30:15: "In quietness and in trust shall be your strength." Unfortunately, even Hezekiah, a good king, was not ready to take God at His Word but entered into an alliance with Egypt for assistance and support. God condemns this lack of trust, 28—31, but still offers a beautiful Messianic promise, 32, and goes on to pronounce judgment on the enemies of Judah, 33—34, and concludes this section with the Messianic prophecy that the ransomed of the Lord "shall obtain joy and gladness, and sorrow and sighing shall flee away," 35.

The next four chapters (Is. 36—39) give historical information about the days of Hezekiah. Parallel accounts are found in 2 Kings 18:13—20:11 and 2 Chron. 32:9-26. Sennacherib, ruler of Assyria, and Rabshakeh, the army general, threatened Jerusalem but were repulsed, Is. 36:1—37:38. Then follows an account of Hezekiah's illness and recovery and the Babylonian visitors, Is. 38:1—39:8.

This concludes the first part of the Book of Isaiah. Many scholars are convinced that this part, usually referred to as the "Assyrian Section," constitutes the part written by Isaiah. They suggest that the second part, the "Babylonian Section," was written by at least one other individual, Deutero-Isaiah, Is. 40—54, or perhaps by two other individuals, Trito-Isaiah, Is. 55—66, or by an Isaianic School of disciples. These scholars usually maintain that the "Babylonian Section" was written much later, after the Jews had returned from the exile. Some of the reasons advanced are these: the vocabulary and style are quite different; an entirely different trend of thought is introduced; the Babylonian Captivity is presupposed; the comfort is applicable to people who lived much later than Isaiah; the specific statements about Cyrus and Jerusalem seem to fit better as historical accounts than as prophecies. Counter arguments can be presented to explain these differences and to support the unity of the book. Regardless of conjectured theories of authorship, the entire Book of Isaiah is inspired by the Holy Spirit and, therefore, totally God's Word of truth for all time. The New Testament quotes Isaiah by name some twenty times and these quotations refer to both sections.

The second major part of the Book of Isaiah, the "Babylonian Section," comprises three evenly balanced cycles, each consisting of three major prophecies and ending with a common refrain, "There is no peace, says my God, for the wicked" Is. 48:22; 57:21; 66:24. The modern division into chapters recognizes these cycles and allots nine chapters to each cycle for a total of twenty-seven. The fifty-third chapter (prophecy of vicarious atonement) is in the center (like a mountain peak) with thirteen chapters before and thirteen chapters after.

The theme of the first cycle, Is. 40—48, is the physical redemption of God's people. Jahweh will redeem Judah from the Babylonian Captivity, for He is the omnipotent and gracious Lord: redemption guaranteed by God's power, 40—42; redemption guaranteed by God's grace, 43—45; exhortation to accept God's grace, 46—48. Special passages in this cycle: God's messenger, 40:1-11; sermon of the stars, 40:26-31; precious comfort, 41:10; cf. 42:1-4 and Matt. 12:18-21; God's presence, 43:1-3; God loves and forgives, 44:21, 22; promise for old age, 46:4; God, our Redeemer, 47:4.

The second cycle, Is. 49—57, unfolds the spiritual redemption. The Suffering Servant of Jahweh will redeem the world from sin: Jahweh will be faithful to His promise and send His Servant for redemption, 49—51; how the Suffering Servant will accomplish the redemption, 52—54; invitation to accept the redemption, 55—57. Significant passages in this cycle: God's tremendous love, 49:10, 13-16; messenger of the Gospel, 52:7; vicarious atonement, 53:1-12; spread the redemption story, 54:2, 5, 7, 8, 10; accept the good news, 55:6-13; cf. 56:8 and John 10:16.

The third cycle, Is. 58—66, describes the unspeakable glory of the Lord's redeemed in time and in eternity: the need of repentance to be able to receive the redemption, 58—60; the glory of God's redemption, 61—63:6; the consummation of it all in the last days, 63:7—66. Meaningful passages to be noted especially: works expressing repentance, Is. 58:7 (Matt. 3:8 and Luke 3:8); the Epiphany picture, Is. 60:1-6; Jesus' first sermon text, Is. 61:1-2 (Luke 4:18-21); trodding the winepress for us, Is. 63:1-3; joy and glory of heaven, Is. 65:17-25 (Rev. 21); penitence opens the door to God's presence, Is. 66:1-2; contrast of heaven and hell, Is. 66:22-24.

The name "Isaiah" means "Jahweh is salvation." Isaiah has been properly called "the Evangelist of the Old Testament" by Jerome, the fifth-century church father who translated the Bible into Latin (the Vulgate). He wrote: "It would be proper to call him (Isaiah), not so much prophet, but rather an evangelist; for he displays before our eyes the mysteries of Christ and the church so clearly that one might think he [was] not writing prophecies of future events but [was] telling the story of past occurrences." There are forty-one different passages of Isaiah quoted explicitly or implicitly in sixty-six passages of the New Testament, more than from any other Old Testament book except the Psalms. Without question Isaiah is preeminent among all the Old Testament literary prophets of God.

The Book of Micah
Micah is often called "Small Isaiah" or "Isaiah in Miniature" because he was a younger contemporary of

Isaiah and his message is very similar to Isaiah's. Is. 2:2-4 and Micah 4:1-3 are identical passages. Micah ("Who is like Jahweh?") is identified as the "Morasthite" or "of Moresheth," a small town about twenty-five miles southwest of Jerusalem, near Gath, a city of the Philistines. He was a prophet of the common people and rural life, while Isaiah was more the court preacher and urban prophet. The kings of Judah, Jotham, Ahaz, and Hezekiah, are mentioned, Micah 1:1; but Micah's message was also directed to Israel and Samaria, soon to be destroyed by the Assyrians. A pertinent reference to Micah is found in Jer. 26:16-19, where certain elders cite the precedent of Hezekiah who did not kill Micah for preaching the Law and through this precedent are seeking to save the life of Jeremiah.

Another interesting allusion to Micah is in the New Testament passage, Matt. 10:35, 36, concerning enmity in families (cf. Micah 7:6). But the most significant reference to Micah is the Messianic prophecy of the birth of Christ in Bethlehem-Ephratah (Micah 5:2; cf. Matt. 2:5, 6, and John 7:42). The incidents related in Matt. 2:5, 6 and in John 7:42 indicate that some Jews who studied the Old Testament understood the Messianic nature of this prophetic passage in Micah 5:2.

The message of Micah can be outlined in various ways. One outline delineates the three discourses, each beginning with the words, "Hear ye," Micah 1:2; 3:1, 6:1. The first speech presents Jahweh's controversy with the two capitals, Jerusalem and Samaria. Both face judgment because of their idolatry, covetousness, oppression, drunkenness, and false teachings, Micah 1:2—2:11; but God will have mercy on a remnant, 2:12-13. The second describes Jahweh's controversy with the rulers, prophets, priests, and princes; because they abuse and mislead the people ("skin" the needy, 3:3), they will be punished, 3:1-12; but God will show marvelous mercy in sending the Everlasting Ruler in Bethlehem, 4:1—5:15.

The third presents Jahweh's controversy with the people. In their ingratitude the people have sunk into a lifeless ritualism in their worship and do not seem to recognize what Jahweh requires of them (Micah 6:8), and thus fail to serve Him properly, 6:1—7:13; but still God in His mercy promises, if they repent, to cast their sins into the depths of the sea, 7:14-20.

Another brief outline is this: Message of punishment, Micah 1:1—2:13; message of promise, 3:1—5:15; message of pardon, 6:1—7:20. A third approach is to view the Book of Micah as a kind of covenant lawsuit of Jahweh against His people. The book begins with the summons, 1:1-2. Jahweh is the plaintiff, Israel and Judah are the defendants, and the mountains are the witnesses. Jahweh steps forth in all His majesty and prefers the indictment, 1:3-5. Then He adduces the evidence by reviewing His dealing with the people and their response through the years. He even asks where He has failed them and invites them to plead their case, 1:6—6:5. Israel answers the indictment with an anemic appeasement offering, 6:6-7. Then Micah suggests a better defense, "He has showed you, O man, what is good; and what does the Lord require of you but to do justice, and to love kindness, and to walk humbly with your God," 6:8. Jahweh passes judgment, 6:9-16. Judah accepts the sentence in penitence and promises to amend her ways and to trust in Jahweh's mercy and faithfulness, 7:1-20.

The Book of Nahum

After Hezekiah's death, his son, Manasseh, became king at the age of twelve. His total reign was longer than that of any king of Judah or Israel, but for a number of those years Manasseh was imprisoned by the Assyrians, 2 Kings 21:1-18 and 2 Chron. 33:1-20. Assyria was so powerful that Manasseh decided his only choice was to pay tribute and to cooperate in every other way that Assyria demanded, even in fostering Assyrian idolatry.

After Manasseh's death, his son, Amon, in his brief reign of two years, followed the same course, 2 Kings 21:19-26 and 2 Chron. 33:21-25.

It was under such circumstances that Nahum was called by God to be His prophet. He is identified as Nahum of Elkosh. Jerome in the fifth century A.D. suggested that this was the village Elkese in Galilee. Others identify it as the village Elkush, north of Nineveh, where some claim to have discovered the tomb of Nahum. Still others refer to Capernaum in Galilee as the "village of Nahum." Most Bible scholars assume that Elkosh was a city in Galilee and that Nahum escaped out of Galilee during the Assyrian invasion and came to the province of Judah where God called him as a prophet.

The name "Nahum" means "comfort" or "the consoler." As the title of the book announces (An oracle concerning Nineveh), the purpose of Nahum is to offer comfort and consolation to God's people by prophesying that Assyria, the world's most powerful kingdom at that time, and Nineveh, the capital, will be utterly destroyed. A note of triumphant joy runs through the entire prophecy because God will avenge the wrongs this wicked nation has committed. Although at the time of Nahum's prophecy Nineveh's destruction seemed unlikely, it occurred as dramatically and drastically as predicted. God even compares the destruction to that which Assyria through Esarhaddon in 669 B.C. and through Ashurbanipal in 663 B.C. had brought upon Thebes (No) in Egypt (cf. Nah. 3:8). By the year 625 B.C. Assyria was caught in a life-and-death struggle. Egypt tried to help but in 614 B.C. the Medes conquered Assyria, and in 612 B.C. Nineveh fell before a coalition of Babylonians, Medes, and Scythians. This is the destruction prophesied by Nahum.

The Book of Nahum is well planned and follows a clear outline: picture of God, the Judge, Nah. 1; execution of the judgment, 2; reason for the judgment, 3.

It can also be presented as two odes: the ode to God's majesty: God's vengeance, 1:1-6; God's grace, 2:7-11; God's restoration of Judah, 1:12—2:2; the ode on the destruction on Nineveh: descriptive prophecy of the siege and fall of Nineveh, 2:3-13; and the cause of the fall, 3:1-19.

The prophecy sweeps along with relentless force as it unerringly proclaims that no one "can stand before His indignation," Nah. 1:6. Yet the comforting assertion is made, "The Lord is good, a stronghold in the day of trouble; He knows those who take refuge in Him," 1:7. Nineveh does not seek the Lord and, therefore, God says, "I will make your grave, for you are vile," 1:14. Then Nahum vividly describes the invading soldiers and the total devastation of the city: "Desolate! Desolation and ruin! Hearts faint and knees tremble," 2:10. God gives the reason for it all: "Woe to the bloody city, all full of lies and booty," 3:1. The prophecy ends in a pitiless note of condemnation: Nineveh has deserved this destruction! "All who hear the news of you clap their hands over you, for upon whom has not come your unceasing evil?" 3:19. At Jonah's preaching, 150 years earlier, Nineveh had repented, but now there was no thought of repentance and so annihilation was inevitable.

The Book of Habakkuk

Amon ruled over Judah for only two years when he was murdered in a "patriotic" revolt. His son, Josiah, who was only eight years old, succeeded him. Josiah was a pious king and in the twelfth year of his reign (629 B.C.) initiated a wide-ranging program of religious reform. Six years later, he ordered a major renovation of the temple to remove all traces of Assyrian and other heathen influences, 2 Kings 22:1-7 and 2 Chron. 34:1-13. In the course of this reconstruction work "the book of the Law" was found. Hilkiah, the priest, gave it to Shaphan, the secretary, who read it to Josiah. He, in turn, was so impressed that he sent the book to Huldah, the prophetess, who verified its authenticity. Consequently, Josiah called an assembly of all the people for a public reading of this "book of the Law." By acclamation, this undergirded a period of national reformation, 2 Kings 22:8—23:25 and 2 Chron. 34:14—35:19. In spite of this encouraging development, the account in 2 Kings 23:26 continues: "Still the Lord did not turn from the fierceness of His great wrath, by which His anger was kindled against Judah, because of all the provocations with which Manasseh had provoked Him."

The historical events just related provide a meaningful background for some of the questions raised in the Book of Habakkuk and also for the renewal of proper temple worship. Biographical data in the book are sketchy. Habakkuk was an inhabitant of the Kingdom of Judah and possibly a Levite. The latter is inferred from the musical and liturgical terms used in chapter 3, which are similar to those in the Psalms (cf. especially Ps. 77:16-21). The name Habakkuk seems to be derived from the term for a Babylonian plant *chambaququ* ("a climbing vine," figurative for "one who embraces," i.e., "one who dearly loves.")

The canonicity of the book is corroborated by these New Testament references: Acts 13:40, 41 (Hab. 1:5); Matt. 24:28 (Hab. 1:8); and the well-known quotation of Hab. 2:4 in Rom. 1:17; Gal. 3:11; and Heb. 10:38. Some scholars conjecture that the third chapter is a later addition since the copy of this book found among the Dead Sea Scrolls contains only the first two chapters. The Septuagint translation, however, includes the third chapter.

The book is clearly divided into three major parts, corresponding to the three chapters: the terrible judgment to come through the Chaldeans, Hab. 1; the five woes with which God threatens Chaldea, Hab. 2; the majestic theophany of God and Habakkuk's response, Hab. 3.

An outline of more immediate application to modern readers is this series of questions and responses relating to life's perennial problems: "Why is God so slow in doing something about all the problems around us?" (Hab. 1:1-4); God acts but not as man expects and then man asks: "God, why do You do what You do in regard to the problems around us?" (1:5-17). God answers the "Why?" as far as God's prople are concerned (2:1-5). Then God answers "Why?" as far as the wicked are concerned (2:6-20). God emphasizes His answer by His Person and by His action, a tremendous theophany (3:1-15). The response of God's people to God's answers and actions is a psalm of praise and trust (3:16-19). The message of the Book of Habakkuk can well be summarized in God's statement of promise: "The righteous shall live by his faith" (2:4) and the prophet's statement of faith, "I will rejoice in the Lord, I will joy in the God of my salvation" (3:18).

The Book of Zephaniah

Zephaniah was a contemporary of Habakkuk. He is the only prophet whose genealogy is traced to four generations: "son of Cushi, son of Gedaliah, son of Amariah, son of Hezekiah," Zeph. 1:1. Was his great-great-grandfather the King Hezekiah? Many Bible scholars assume that this is the Hezekiah mentioned here. Others, however, express doubt for the following reasons: Hezekiah was a rather common name; if this Hezekiah was the king, his title would have been used; it was customary to add the title whenever a king was introduced for the first time in a document.

Zephaniah prophesied during the early years of Josiah's reign. If Josiah had already begun his reform at the time Zephaniah prophesied, the people had not yet reacted in any noticeable manner. This book, which seems to be a summary of Zephaniah's messages, is exceedingly somber in its tone and is filled with threatenings and denunciations, similar to the Book of Amos. But the sun breaks through the clouds in the last chapter in the prophecy of the coming of a happy day when God's people will lift their voices in praise and thanksgiving.

The Book of Zephaniah is one continuous discourse with the three basic elements found in other prophetic writings: (1) judgments against Judah; (2) judgments against other nations; (3) promises for Judah's future restoration. A favorite term is "day of wrath" (inspiration for the medieval Latin hymn "Dies Irae") or "day of the Lord" (Zeph. 1:7, 8, 14, 15, 16, 18 and 2:2, 3). This last verse, Zeph. 2:3: "perhaps you may be hidden on the day of wrath," relates to the meaning of the name "Zephaniah" ("Jahweh hides"), indicating God's gracious protection of His people.

The general theme of the book is "Certainty of God's Day of Wrath on the Impenitent." Part I: Universality of God's Judgment (Zeph. 1:2—3:7): upon earth, sky, and sea, 1:2, 3; upon Judah, 1:4-18; call to repentance, 2:1-3; judgment upon Gentile nations: Philistia 2:4-7; Moab and Ammon, 2:8-11; the Cushites, 2:12; Assyria, 2:13-15; God's judgment upon Judah repeated, 3:1-7. Part II: Universality of God's Grace upon All People (Zeph 3:8-20): Gentiles and Jews united into one holy church, 3:8-13; joyous activity on earth and in heaven, 3:14-20. The closing verse of the book is a sweeping promise of restoration and hope: "At that time I will bring you home, at the time when I gather you together; yea, I will make you renowned and praised among all the peoples of the earth, when I restore your fortunes before your eyes, says the Lord," 3:20.

Zephaniah often uses expressions previously used by other prophets, e.g., Zeph. 1:7 (Joel 1:15 and 2:31); Zeph.

3:13 (Is. 34:16); Zeph. 1:14, 15 (Joel 2:1, 2). The canonicity of the book is established.

The Book of Jeremiah

The Book of Jeremiah portrays a prophet as a paradox: he seems to be shy and of extremely mild temperament personally but unusually courageous and bold in his official duties; he is regarded as a traitor because he suggests yielding to the Babylonians since their victory is certain, but he proves to be a loyal patriot by staying in Jerusalem although offered rescue and escape; he is called "the weeping prophet," yet he demonstrates superb manliness in the face of ridicule and even persecution.

Jeremiah was a young man, the son of a priest, Hilkiah, in Anathoth, a few miles northwest of Jerusalem, when God called him to be a prophet, Jer. 1:4-10. This call came to Jeremiah in the thirteenth year of the reign of King Josiah (626 B.C.). Jeremiah continued to serve as God's prophet in Jerusalem until the end of the reign of Zedekiah, the last king of Judah (586 B.C.), and even under the rule of the governor, Gedaliah, appointed by the Babylonians. When Gedaliah was murdered by the Jews, the murderers forced Jeremiah to flee with them to Egypt. Tradition relates that Jeremiah suffered martyrdom in Egypt. He has been called "the martyr of the prophet's office." Origen said of him that "he was long a martyr before he actually became a martyr in death." He suffered one disappointment and hardship after another: he preached against idol worship, but the people boasted of the good they received from idols (Jer. 44:15-18); he wrote his prophecies in a book, but King Jehoiakim cut it up and burned it (Jer. 36:23); he was forbidden ever to marry (Jer. 16:1, 2); the people cursed him (Jer. 15:10); threatened to kill him (Jer. 26:8); and even threw him into a dungeon to die (Jer. 38:6).

As long as Josiah was king, Jeremiah could count on

his support. But in 609 B.C. Pharaoh Necho of Egypt marched through Palestine on his way to join forces with Assyria. King Josiah attempted to stop Pharaoh Necho at Megiddo but was killed, and the people of Judah were thrown into a state of frustration and confusion, 2 Kings 23:29-30 and 2 Chron. 35:20-27.

After Josiah's death, the people did not place his oldest son, Eliakim (Jehoiakim), on the throne but chose Jehoahaz (Shallum), the second oldest son, as king. Pharaoh Necho resented this action and removed Jehoahaz after only three months' rule and sent him to Egypt where he died. Then Necho made Eliakim king, changed his name to Jehoiakim, and imposed a heavy tribute on the people. Jehoiakim was an irresponsibly wicked king, so that at his death God forbade the people to lament for him and told them to have him "cast forth beyond the gates of Jerusalem" (Jer. 22:19). After Jehoiakim's death, his son, Jehoiachin, ruled three months and ten days. Because he had aroused the distrust of King Nebuchadnezzar of Babylon, who had defeated Assyria and was now in control of the Fertile Crescent, Jehoiachin was deported with more than ten thousand leaders of Judah to Babylon in 597 B.C. In Jehoiachin's place, his uncle, Zedekiah (Mattaniah), the youngest son of Josiah, was made king by Nebuchadnezzar. He was ambiguous and vacillating in his attitude toward Jeremiah. He asked the prophet for advice and requested Jeremiah's prayers in his behalf, yet he imprisoned him and subjected him to cruel treatment. In the year 586 B.C. Nebuchadnezzar destroyed Jerusalem. When Zedekiah tried to escape, he was captured and brought before Nebuchadnezzar at Riblah. His sons were killed in his presence; then he was blinded, placed in chains, and deported to Babylon, 2 Kings 23:31—25:7 and 2 Chron. 36:1-21.

The arrangement of the Book of Jeremiah is more topical than chronological. It may be divided into two major sections, Jer. 2—45 containing chiefly prophecies and narratives about Judah and Jerusalem; and Jer. 46—51 consisting of predictions of judgment against nine foreign nations. The first chapter is introductory and the last (52) seems to be an epilog, possibly added by Baruch, Jeremiah's secretary. There are five major emphases in the book: (1) Judah will be taken into exile by Babylon; (2) Judah's repentance will bring God's favor and blessing; (3) Judah's yielding to Babylon will diminish her grief; (4) Judah, though captured, will return after seventy years and under the new covenant will become the New Testament church destined to guide the world; (5) Babylon, Judah's captor, will be utterly destroyed, an illustration of the significance of the name "Jeremiah" ("Jahweh flings down").

One general outline of the Book of Jeremiah is the following: Jeremiah's call: personal, Jer. 1:1-10, official (almond rod, seething pot) 1:11-19. Reasons for the fall of Jerusalem: character of God's people: ingratitude, 2—6; formalism, 7—9; idolatry, 10—11; character of God: just punishment upon the impenitent, 12—13; faithful support of the preaching of His prophet, 14—17. Illustration of authority to effect the fall: pottery molded, 18, and pottery shattered, 19.

The prophecies of judgment and captivity are fulfilled: against the leaders: priests, Jer. 20; kings, 21 and 22; prophets, 23; against the people, symbol of figs, 24; character of the judgment, 25 and 26:7; adverse reaction of people, 26:8—29:32. Glorious promise is made of return and future blessings, 30—33, especially the prophecy of the new covenant, 31:31-34. Specific incidents are reported during the captivity siege: definite prophecy of downfall, 34; the example of the Rechabites, 35; Jehoiakim's destruction of Jeremiah's writings, 36; Zedekiah's request for prayers, 37:1-10; Jeremiah's imprisonment and release, 37:11 and 38:28; and the capture of Jerusalem, 39. Incidents which occurred after the siege: Gedaliah made governor, 40—41; Jeremiah's plea not to force him to go to Egypt, 42; plea goes unheeded and Jeremiah is forced to go to Egypt, 43 and 44. God has a word of promise for Baruch, 45.

God's prophecies are announced through Jeremiah against the foreign nations: Egypt, Jer. 46; Philistia, 47; Moab, 48; Ammon, Edom, Damascus, Kedar, Hazor, Elam, 49; Babylon, 50 and 51. Recapitulation of the account of the fall of Jerusalem, the capture of Judah, the doom of Zedekiah, and the release of Jehoiachin from prison in Babylonia, 52.

Jeremiah announces Messianic hopes and prophecies in various ways. Numerous quotations and allusions are found in the New Testament, e.g., Jer. 7:11 (Matt. 21:13, Luke 19:46); Jer. 9:23, 24 (1 Cor. 1:29, 31); Jer. 31:1, 9, 33 (2 Cor. 6:16, 18); Jer. 31:15 (Matt. 2:17, 18); Jer. 31:31-34 (Heb. 8:8-12; Heb. 10:16, 17). These help to establish the canonicity of this book.

The Book of Lamentations

In 2 Chron. 35:25 the statement is made that "Jeremiah also uttered a lament for Josiah." It was customary practice among the Jews to compose dirges or elegies not only at the loss of loved ones but also when cities were devastated and nations were conquered (cf. Amos 5:1, 2; Ezek. 26:17). The Septuagint carries this superscription for the Book of Lamentations: "And it came to pass that after Israel had been taken captive and Jerusalem had been destroyed, Jeremiah sat down weeping and composed the following Song of Lamentations over Jerusalem and said . . . ." Therefore, Jews and Christians alike have regarded Jeremiah as the writer of this book.

In the Hebrew Bible it carries the title, "O how!" (cf. Lam. 1:1). The Septuagint entitles it "Dirges" and the Vulgate, "Lamentations." In the original Hebrew text chapters 1, 2, 4, and 5 each have 22 verses corresponding to the 22 letters of the Hebrew alphabet. Chapter 3 has 66 verses in which every three verses begin with a letter of the alphabet in sequence from beginning to end. All chapters, except the last, are in the form of an alphabetical acrostic. This book is read annually by the Jews in its entirety at the festival commemorating the destruction of Jerusalem. As one reads the book, the pathetic and pitiful condition of Jerusalem becomes very vivid and real. At the same time one hears inspiring expressions of comfort and hope, cf. Lam. 3:22, 23; 3:25, 26; 3:32, 33.

The following outline marks the progress of thought in the book: a lament for the fallen city: description of her desolation, Lam. 1:1-11 and a confession of her sin, 1:12-22; the reason for her fall: the Lord's judgment, 2:1-13; her false prophets, 2:14-22; the reason for her hope: sympathy of the prophet in her suffering, 3:1-21; the never-failing mercy of God, 3:22-36; trust in God's justice, 3:37-54; and the prophet's prayers in her behalf, 3:55-66; a vivid description of the siege: the resulting grief, 4:1-12; the helplessness of the false prophets, 4:13-16; the lack of a foreign ally, 4:17-20; warning to Edom, 4:21; hope of rescue, 4:22; a prayer for mercy, 5:1-6; confession of misery and guilt, 5:7-18; plea for mercy, 5:19-22.

Modern scholarship has raised questions about the traditional assumption that Jeremiah wrote the Book of Lamentations and for a number of different reasons. There are, however, as many arguments in favor of Jeremiah's authorship as there are to place it in doubt. The important consideration here, as with all canonical books, is the divine inspiration of the Holy Spirit, which gives assurance of its authenticity and authority for the faith and life of Christians today.

5

The Period of the Exile

The Book of Daniel

Just as Isaiah, Habakkuk, and Jeremiah had prophesied, that God would permit the Babylonians to carry the Jews into captivity, so it happened late in the seventh century before Christ. Even before Jerusalem was captured and destroyed, Babylonia started to take some Jews into exile. The Babylonians followed the practice of the Assyrians with conquered nations. They expatriated the healthy, intelligent, and high regarded citizens to serve as their slaves, and they left those who had defects in the homeland.

The first captives taken to Babylon "in the third year of the reign of Jehoiakim, king of Judah," Dan. 1:1 (606 B.C.), included four gifted youths: Daniel, Hananiah, Mishael, and Azariah, Dan. 1:7. Of these, Daniel rose to greatest prominence in Babylon and this book bears his name. It is different from all other Old Testament books (except Ezekiel) because of its apocalyptic character. The word "apocalyptic" is derived from a Greek term meaning "to uncover, to disclose." But, in reality, apocalyptic literature is often rather obscure because the style is typically cryptic with extraordinary visions, strange symbols, and supernatural happenings. This is by design, for the true meaning of the message is intended only for the select few and to be hidden from the enemy. Consequently, the inherent ambiguity of such a style gives rise to some weird and extravagant interpretations and applications of the Book of Daniel and of its New Testament counterpart, the Book of Revelation.

Many modern Bible scholars do not regard Daniel as the author, nor do they date the book in the period of the Babylonian Captivity but much later, probably in the second century before Christ at the time of the activity of the Maccabees. They attribute the authorship to one of the Hasidim ("loyal or pious ones"), the forerunners of the later Pharisees, on the assumption that the writer wanted to encourage the Jews to remain faithful and loyal to their heritage. For this reason he recalled for their imitation the example of Daniel, the great hero of Jewish tradition, who remained faithful to Jahweh even in a foreign land in the face of numerous dangers, temptations, and threats.

Some of the arguments advanced in support of this view are these: supposedly inaccurate historical statements, e.g., confusion about the kings mentioned; bilingual nature of the book (Dan. 1 and 8—12 are Hebrew and Dan. 2:4—7:28 are Aramaic); inappropriate expressions of self-praise, cf., Dan. 1:17, 19, 20; 3:11, 12; 6:4; 9:23; 10:11; the prophecies give the impression of being accounts of past occurrences rather than predictions of future events; and in the original Hebrew Bible this book was not placed among the Nebi'im (Prophets) but with the Kethubim (Sacred Writings). For a thorough discussion of the arguments supporting either the earlier or the later view of the time of writing, the reader is referred to the pertinent books in the bibliography.

The historicity of Daniel as a person is affirmed by references to him in Ezek. 14:14, 20 and 28:3, and by Christ in Matt. 24:15. The message of the book certainly fits the entire emphasis of the Holy Scriptures, namely, that in spite of evil and ungodly powers at work in the world, God always remains in control both in the life of individuals and in the destiny of nations and especially in the protection of His church. The comforting Messianic prophecies (Dan. 2:44; and 7:13, 14) anticipate the future blessings for the church in New Testament times.

Daniel seems to have been a descendant of a Jewish family of high, perhaps even of royal, rank. He was a young man, between the ages of 15 and 20, when he was forcibly removed from Jerusalem to Babylon. His name was changed in Babylon from Daniel ("God is my Judge") to Belteshazzar ("Bel, protect his life"). Strangely enough, however, the book usually refers to him by his Jewish name, whereas his three young friends are more commonly identified by their Babylonian names: Hananiah ("God is gracious"), changed to Shadrach ("command of Aku," an idol); Michael ("Who is as God is?") to Meshach ("Who is as Aku is?"); and Azariah ("Jahweh is a helper") to Abednego ("slave of Nabu," an idol). Daniel gained high recognition during his long period of service at the court, first under the Babylonian kings, then the Median governor, Darius, and finally the Persian king, Cyrus. He did not return to Jerusalem when Cyrus released the Jews from captivity but remained in Babylon. He must have reached at least the age of ninety before he died. God gave him the promise, "Go your way till the end; and you shall rest, and shall stand at your allotted place at the end of the days," Dan. 12:13.

The Book of Daniel is divided into two major sections of six chapters each: Part I presents historical events in the life of Daniel, 1—6; Part II unfolds the visions relating to the kingdoms of the world and the Messiah, seen by Daniel and interpreted by angels, 7—12. The unity of the book is evident in the inner connection between chapters of the first part to others in the second part, e.g. Dan. 2 and 7; 5 and 8; 6 and 9.

One outline of the book presents God as the Ruler of the state in Part I and as the ruler of the church in Part II. Part I: Dan. 1: God's providence as Daniel and his friends begin their political career in Babylon; 2: God's help in interpreting the king's dream and the resulting political advancement; 3: God's guardian care of the spiritual and physical welfare of Daniel's friends; 4: God's interpretation and fulfillment of the king's dream of a tree; 5: God's interpretation and fulfillment of the handwriting on the wall; 6: God's guardian care of the spiritual and physical welfare of Daniel. Part II: 7: God's interpretation of the vision of the four beasts and the Son of Man in relation to the history of God's people; 8: God's application of the vision of the ram (Persia) and the he-goat (Greece) to the future history of God's people; 9: Daniel's confession and prayer (vs. 1-19) and Gabriel's revelation of God's time through the vision of the seventy weeks; 10—12: vision of the last times—God will use angels to help man fight his battles, 10:1—11, 1; nations rise and fall at God's will, 11:2-45; Michael will deliver God's people from all their tribulations until the end of days, 12:1-13.

Another outline may make the book more directly relevant and appealing to modern readers: God blesses godly children and youths, Dan. 1:1-21; God controls the destinies of nations, 2:1-49 and 7:1-28; God shows the contrast of His action toward the godly and the ungodly, 3:1-30 and 4:1-37; God reveals to the godly the doom of the ungodly, 8:1-27 and 5:1-31; God always takes care of the godly, 9:1-27 and 6:1-28; God gives personal assurance to the godly of loving concern for all time, 10:1—11:45; God has great blessings in store for the godly, 12:1-13. The comprehensive promise of 12:3 applies to all of God's people for all time: "Those who are wise shall shine as the brightness of the firmament; and those who turn many to righteousness like the stars forever and ever."

The Book of Ezekiel

Nine years after Daniel and his friends had been carried away to Babylonia, there was another invasion of

Jerusalem (597 B.C.), and this time King Jehoiachin and Ezekiel ("God is strong"), the son of the priest Buzi, were taken into captivity together with other prominent citizens of Jerusalem, Ezek. 1:1-3; 33:21; 40:1; 2 Kings 24:10-16; 2 Chron. 36:9, 10.

Ezekiel's Babylonian home was by the Chebar River, a ship canal which branched off from the Euphrates about fifty miles above Babylon. At that time Babylon was one of the most beautiful cities of the world, filled with palaces, gardens, temples, and protected by massive walls. The colony of Jewish exiles with whom Ezekiel lived was located at Tel-abib, Ezek. 3:15. Daniel had already attained a high position in the palace of Nebuchadnezzar, and some of the other Jews, as excavations of business documents in this area have revealed, were doing well in business ventures. Ezekiel was married (24:18) and lived in his own house (8:1).

When Ezekiel had been in Babylon five years, God called him to be a prophet (592 B.C.). He tells about his commissioning in the first person (Ezek. 1:4—3:27). In a rather strange and complex vision of stormy wind, flashing fire, four living creatures (faces of man, lion, ox, and eagle), wheels, and a resplendent throne, God demonstrated His majesty and His control over all creation. He told Ezekiel that many of the people would refuse to listen to his message (2:3-10) but earnestly laid upon his conscience the burden of being a faithful and responsible "watchman for the house of Israel" (3:16-27).

The first five to six years were very difficult for Ezekiel. Some of the people were disgusted and homesick in exile (Ps. 137). Others felt God had treated the Jews unjustly by even permitting any heathen nation to take them into captivity, and others did not believe the Lord would ever permit Jerusalem, and especially not Solomon's temple, to be destroyed. They were getting reports that conditions in Jerusalem were quite normal and, therefore, they thought that both Jeremiah in

Jerusalem and Ezekiel in Babylonia were simply trying to frighten them with their stern preaching.

The first twenty-four chapters of the book (Ezek. 1—24) present the *presiege* period of Ezekiel's prophecies, in which he consistently predicts that the destruction of Jerusalem will come. The next eight chapters (25—32) announce God's judgment on foreign nations. The last sixteen chapters (33—48) prophesy of *postsiege* conditions, depicting the restoration, especially the new temple and the new Jerusalem, as symbols of the New Testament church. After 586 B.C. when the temple was destroyed, the people gave much more credibility to Ezekiel's preaching, and he became highly respected among the elders of the Jews in Babylon, 8:1; 14:1; 20:1.

Because of certain statements in Ezek. 8—11, some Biblical scholars assume that Ezekiel spent some of his prophetic career in Jerusalem. Others contend that he merely fancied his visions as actual experiences and, therefore, they draw the conclusion that he was physically not present in Jerusalem. Opinions also vary about the arrangement and style of the book. Some regard Ezekiel as highly educated, remarkably eloquent, extraordinarily imaginative, and well organized. Others think that his writings show him to have been pedantic, repetitious, confused, and even bizarre. The Christian Bible student who accepts the entire book as inspired by the Holy Ghost may not always be able to understand or interpret all the symbolic illustrations and actions of Ezekiel. He will, however, certainly stand in awe of God's majesty, justice, and love as portrayed in this prophetic book, and will agree with the judgment of Jerome that it is "an ocean and labyrinth of the mysteries of God."

Ezekiel continued in his prophetic career for at least twenty-two years, until the twenty-seventh year of his captivity and the seventeenth year after the destruction of Jerusalem (570 B.C.), Ezek. 29:17. Nothing of a reliable nature is known about his later years and death. An old tradition relates that Ezekiel had contact with Pythagoras (582—500 B.C.?), the Greek philosopher and mathematician, founder of a religous brotherhood, who postulated an orderly universe of mathematical proportion and delved into the mysteries of life and death and reincarnation, but perhaps best known for the Pythagorean theorem. The authenticity and integrity of the book are generally acknowledged, although some scholars contend there is evidence of editing by someone besides Ezekiel. The consistent use of the first person (exceptions Ezek. 1:3 and 24:24) patently attests to Ezekiel's authorship. These New Testament references corroborate the canonical character of the book: Ezek. 34:23 (John 10:12; 1 Pet. 2:25); Ezek. 36:23 (Rom 2:24); Ezek. 38 (Rev. 20:8, God and Magog); Ezek. 37:27; 40:2, 3, 5; 48:31-35 (Rev. 21:3, 10, 12, 15, 16); Ezek. 47:1, 12 (Rev. 22:1, 2).

The Book of Ezekiel is a "theodicy," defense of God, justifying His dealing with Judah. It contains many parables and extended proverbs (Ezek. 12:22-25; 16:44-63; 17:1-10; 18:2-24), also some poetry (19:2-14; 27:3-9; 32:2-8), and a great number of visions, often in the apocalyptic style of the last chapters of the Book of Daniel. Three favorite expressions in the book are: "I am the Lord" (73 times), "son of man" (90 times), and "rebellious house" (17 times).

This is a brief outline of the book: Ezekiel's commission, Ezek. 1—3; the fall of Jerusalem predicted, 4—24; the doom of Gentile nations, 25—32; the restoration of Judah, 33—39; the new dispensation for the Jews after the captivity, 40—48.

A more detailed outline may be helpful in reading the book: I. Ezekiel's commission (592 B.C.), including visions of living creatures and wheels, Ezek. 1, and God's message, equipment, and responsibility, 2—3. II. A. The fall of Jerusalem: predicted and described by symbols (mimic siege, 390-day fasting, 390-day food, shaving and cutting of hair) 4—5; by direct message (against

Jerusalem, 6, against Judah, 7); by visions (idolatry in
temple, 8; inkhorn, 9; coals of fire and cherubim, 10;
wickedness of princes, death of Pelatiah, 11). II. B. The
fall of Jerusalem justified, (1) by exposing the people's
unbelief: false security, 12; false prophets and
prophetesses, 13; hypocrisy of the elders, 14; uselessness of
a vine, 15; weakness of a foundling, 16; false trust in
armies, 17; misunderstanding of God's righteousness,
18—19; and (2) by announcing God's holy purpose: desire
to change idolatrous people to a worshiping and serving
community, 20; plan to hallow God's people through
chastisement: forest fire and song of the sword, 21; silver
melted by fire, 22; harlots, Oholah and Oholibah,
severely punished, 23; boiling pot and woe beyond
mourning, 24.

III. The doom of Gentile nations and the reasons for
it: Ammon for mocking Judah; Moab for rejoicing over
Judah's fall; Edom for revenge; Philistia for expressing
old hatreds, Ezek. 25; Tyre for insults to Jerusalem, 26,
and for pride in its own wealth, 27:1—28:19; Sidon for
not acknowledging God, 28:20-26; and Egypt for
treachery and pride, 29—32.

IV. The promises of Judah's restoration: the
prophet's serious responsibility, Ezek. 33; the Good
Shepherd, 34; the restored land, 35:1—36:15; a new heart,
36:16-38; a revival of "the dry bones" and a reunion of
"the sticks," 37; defeat of the last enemies, Gog and
Magog, 38—39.

V. Restored order for the Jews as a symbolic picture
of the New Testament church: A. the new temple, the
courts and gateways, Ezek. 40:1-47; the temple proper,
40:48—41:26; the priests' chambers, 42:1-14; measuring
the temple area, 42:15-20; B. the return of Jahweh to the
temple, 43; C. the new priesthood, 44; D. the new
provisions for priests and princes, 45:1-8, and the new
provision for sacrifices and worship, 45:9—46:24; E.
promising picture of future fertility of the land, 47:1-12;

102

extension of the boundaries, 47:13-23; and specific allotments of land, 48. The last sentence of the book must have filled the people of God with hopeful and joyful anticipation for a bright and blessed future: "And the name of the city henceforth shall be, The Lord is there!"

6

The Post-Exilic Period

Introduction

After Ezekiel completed his prophetic ministry, there is no record of an officially called prophet of God in the land of exile. Daniel, of course, continued to be a firm and faithful witness to the true God in his position at the court of the kings of Babylon. It seems, however, that in his old age Daniel's influence had greatly waned. When the strange handwriting appeared on the wall during the great feast which King Belshazzar was hosting for a thousand of his lords, no one could find an interpreter until the queen mother suggested Daniel. From the questions Belshazzar asked Daniel, it is obvious he did not know him, Dan. 5:10-16. The handwriting on the wall read, "MENE, MENE, TEKEL, UPHARSIN," which Daniel interpreted to mean that the days of the Babylonian kingdom were numbered (MENE) because it had not "measured up" to expectations (TEKEL), and the Medes and Persians would conquer Babylon (UP-HARSIN). That very night Belshazzar was killed and the Medes and Persians conquered Babylon (539 B.C.). At first Darius the Mede was placed in charge. It was under his regime that Daniel was cast into the lions' den because he openly defied the edict of Darius forbidding prayer to any god or man except to him, Dan. 6. Shortly thereafter King Cyrus of Persia personally took over the rule of Babylonia.

The prophet Isaiah by divine inspiration had prophesied that Cyrus would be God's instrument to bring the Jews back from Babylon to Jerusalem, Is. 44:28 and 45:1, and the prophet Jeremiah had told them this would happen after seventy years in exile, Jer. 29:10-14. The Second Book of Chronicles closes and the Book of Ezra begins with the account that "in the first year of Cyrus king of Persia" Jeremiah's prophecy was fulfilled when Cyrus issued the proclamation allowing and even encouraging the Jews to return to Jerusalem, 2 Chron. 36:22-23 and Ezra 1:1. There is some confusion in establishing the exact chronology because some scribes used Tishri (fall to fall) reckoning and others used Nisan (spring to spring), and some even used both interchangeably. Accordingly, some consider the first year of Cyrus to be from the fall of 538 B.C. to the fall of 537 B.C., and others calculate the period to be from the spring of 537 B.C. to the spring of 536 B.C. The seventy-year period is, therefore, either 607 to 537 B.C. or 606 to 536 B.C., a period of seventy years, even as God had prophesied through Jeremiah.

The Book of Ezra

The Book of Ezra and the Book of Nehemiah were one book in the Hebrew canon and were kept as such in the Talmud and in the Septuagint. Jerome divided the two and designated the present Book of Nehemiah as the Second Book of Ezra. Modern scholarship regards the two as one and, because of the similarity of style in these two books and in Chronicles, combines all of these into one large historical work, written by an unknown "chronicler."

Questions have been raised about the unity of the Book of Ezra because it obviously has two distinct parts relating events of widely separated time periods. The first (Ezra 1—6) tells the story of the Jews' return from the exile at the time of Cyrus and gives an account of the rebuilding of the temple in Jerusalem (536 B.C. to 516 B.C.). The second (Ezra 7—10) tells of Ezra's coming to Jerusalem and of reforms instituted by him in cooperation with Nehemiah (456 to ca. 540 B.C.). Other questions pertain to the accessibility of the various documents referred to by the author, e.g., Ezra 4:11; 4:17; 5:6; 6:2; 7:11; 8:1; 10:18; and to the Aramaic section which extends from 4:7 to 6:18.

Arguments in favor of Ezra as the author of the entire book are the biographical data and the extensive use of the first person reserved for the second part, relating events in which Ezra was actively involved, the similarity of expressions in both parts, and the fact that Jewish tradition regarded Ezra as the author of the entire book.

Ezra was a priest with an illustrious ancestry (Ezra 7:1-5) and a well-versed scribe (7:6). He seems to have enjoyed the full confidence of King Artaxerxes (7:6 and 7:25, 26). Tradition credits Ezra with identifying the books to be included in the canon of the Old Testament Scriptures. There is no firm evidence to substantiate this claim but Ezra 7:10 indicates the positive attitude of the prophet toward God's Word: "For Ezra had set his heart to study the Law of the Lord, and to do it, and to teach His statutes and ordinances in Israel."

The events in the first part of the Book of Ezra (1—6) occurred in a period of eighty to sixty years before Ezra came to Jerusalem (536/516 B.C. to 456 B.C.). The proclamation of Cyrus, as reported in 2 Chron. 36:23 and in Ezra 1:2-4, reads as though Cyrus was consciously doing this in direct obedience to God's explicit command. It is doubtful that this was Cyrus' motivation, for his policy with captives generally was different from that of the Assyrians and Babylonians. The latter expatriated the strongest and wisest men to their country, but Cyrus felt that this reduced the tribute and other returns too greatly, so it was his policy to leave the leaders in their native country, supervise them carefully, and collect a richer return. The proclamation approving the Jews' return to Jerusalem fits into that pattern.

Not all the Jews were ready to go back to Jerusalem. Ezra gives a rather detailed listing and reports that less than 50,000 returned, Ezra 2:1-70. Excavations in modern times have revealed that many of the Jews were established in business operations in Babylonia and for that reason, presumably, saw no advantage in returning to Jerusalem. Others may have been concerned about the difficulties the first returnees would encounter and decided to wait. Still others, perhaps, had lost their religious zeal and were content to spend the rest of their days in Babylon.

It is, however, very encouraging to see that the chastisement of the exile produced some commendable positive results among God's people: the most striking benefit was the extinction of gross idolatry; religious education in the Torah was advanced through the establishment of synagogs (schools to study and discuss God's Word); and the longing for the promised Messiah was deepened. This change for the better in religious attitudes explains the first major project which the returned captives undertook, namely, the rebuilding of the temple in Jerusalem (Ezra 3:1-13). There were two leaders: Jeshua, the priest, in spiritual matters, and Zerubbabel as the secular leader. Zerubbabel was a descendant of Jehoiachin, the deported King of Judah who was released from prison in Babylon, 2 Kings 25:27-30.

When the inhabitants of Jerusalem and the surrounding territory noticed the reconstruction work, they slandered the Jews in a message to the king of Persia warning that the Jews with their temple and city rebuilt would rebel. An order was given to stop the construction and all building operation on the temple site ceased for the next fifteen years (535 B.C. to 520 B.C.) "until the second year of the reign of Darius, king of Persia" (520 B.C.), Ezra 4:1-23.

Ezra introduces two prophets, Haggai and Zechariah, called by God in 520 B.C. to urge the people to finish rebuilding the temple. Opposition developed again but was not supported by Darius, and the temple was finally completed four years later (516 B.C.), Ezra 5:1—6:22. The last four chapters (7—10) tell of Ezra's personal immigration to Jerusalem (ca. 456 B.C.) at the encouragement of Artaxerxes Longimanus (7:1—8:36) and the work of his reformation, particularly in regard to "mixed marriages" between Jews and members of Gentile tribes and nations (9:1—10:44). The book ends with the statement: "All these had married foreign women, and they put them away with their children."

The Book of Haggai

In Ezra 5:1 the historical statement is made: "Now the prophets, Haggai and Zechariah, the son of Iddo, prophesied to the Jews who were in Judah and Jerusalem, in the name of the God of Israel who was over them." The Scriptures supply no further biographical information about Haggai. No record of his family or his prophetic call has been preserved. Even the meaning of his name, "festive" or "festival," gives no clue to his background. It has been suggested that his name may indicate that he was born on the day of a Jewish festival.

His book is very short, containing only 38 verses. It records four short but emphatic addresses which evidently brought the desired results. They were delivered during the last months (September to December) of 520 B.C., the second year of Darius Hystaspes. The objective of Haggai's messages was primarily practical: to urge the Jews to resume and complete the rebuilding of the temple in Jerusalem which had been interrupted fifteen years earlier (535 B.C.) by the opposition of the people who were occupying the land when the Jews returned from exile.

Haggai made it unmistakably plain that he had a message directly from God through expressions like the following: "the Word of the Lord came by Haggai the prophet," Hag. 1:1; 2:1; 2:10; 2:20; "thus says the Lord of hosts," 1:2, 5, 7, 9; 2:4, 6, 8, 11, 23. Practically no questions have been raised about the authenticity and integrity of the book. Quotation from and allusion to Hag. 2:6 in Heb. 12:26-28 in the New Testament support its canonicity.

In the first address Haggai strongly denounced the indolence and lack of concern of the Jews in their attitude and action toward the rebuilding of the temple. He told the people there was a close relation between their precarious economic and agricultural conditions and their neglect of God's house while they lived in fine, paneled homes, Hag. 1:1-11. Zerubbabel and Joshua (Jeshua in the Book of Ezra) must have applied Haggai's message to themselves and thereby they were aroused to lead the people to action, 1:12-15.

Some of the older generation had either seen Solomon's temple before the exile or had vivid pictures of it from their parents' description of it. They expressed disappointment at the contrast with the temple under construction, Hag. 2:1-3. In his second address a month later, Haggai tried to fire the people's imaginations with the dream of a temple whose glory would far outshine that of Solomon's. The reference to this address in Heb. 12:26-28 demonstrates that "the temple" would be the New Testament church, Hag. 2:4-9. The phrase "the treasures of all nations," 2:7, does not refer to the Messiah Himself but to those chosen by God and brought to faith in Him.

In the third address, delivered two months after the second, Haggai exposed the dead formalism of the worship led by the priests, Hag. 2:10-14. He challenged them to sincere social welfare action with the promise of definite blessings, 2:15-19.

The fourth address was directed to Zerubbabel, the governor of Judah. God honored him by calling him, "My servant," and by establishing him as a "signet," a seal guaranteeing to God's people the fulfillment of His promise given to David (cf. 2 Sam. 7:12-16), Hag. 2:20-23. God's gracious and powerful providence is evident here in His prophetic promise that Zerubbabel will be an important link in that chain of ancestors extending from King David to Jesus Christ, the King of kings (cf. Matt. 1:12 and Luke 3:27), and the Cornerstone of the glorious New Testament temple of God, the holy Christian church.

The Book of Zechariah

Ezra mentions Haggai and Zechariah together as prophets who "prophesied to the Jews who were in Judah and Jerusalem," Ezra 5:1. This corresponds to what is recorded by the prophets themselves. Haggai states he received his call "in the second year of Darius, the king, in the sixth month," Hag. 1:1, and Zechariah writes, "In the eighth month, in the second year of Darius, the Word of the Lord came to Zechariah," Zech. 1:1. Both of these prophets had the same primary objective: the completion of the reconstruction of the temple. Haggai stressed the practical aspects and Zechariah pictured the symbolic and spiritual implications.

The name "Zechariah" means "Jahweh remembers." There are several other Old Testament personalities that carried the same name, cf. 2 Chron. 24:20 (Matt. 23:35); 2 Chron. 26:5; Is. 8:2. The prophet is further identified as the son of Berechiah and the grandson of Iddo. It seems that Berechiah died before Iddo, his father, which would account for the fact that Ezra and Nehemiah mention only Iddo and omit Berechiah's name, cf. Ezra 5:1; Neh.

12:16. No definite information is available regarding the extent of Zechariah's ministry both as a priest and as a prophet. The last dated prophecy in his book was spoken in the fourth year of Darius, 519 B.C., Zech. 7:1. Some have assumed, on the basis of Neh. 12:16, 26, that he was still active in the days of Nehemiah, but that text does not refer to the priests but to the Levites named in Neh. 12:22-25.

Jewish and Christian scholars alike regarded Zechariah as the author of this book until 1644 A.D., when Hugo Grotius expressed doubt about Zechariah as the writer of chapters 9—14. Grotius contended there was strong evidence that these six chapters were written several hundred years later by one or several other authors. Subsequently, many different theories regarding the authorship of chapters 9—14 have been advanced. Critical scholarship is united in ascribing the first eight chapters to Zechariah. Some of the reasons mentioned in support of a Deutero-Zechariah or even a Trito-Zechariah as the author of chapters 9—14 are these: difference in content, visions and prophecies; differences in language and style; mention of Greeks as enemies (Zech. 9:13); ascribing the prophecy about a purchase of a potter's field to Jeremiah in Matt. 27:9 rather than to Zechariah, cf. Zech. 11:12 f. Scholars are not agreed on these reasons nor on the various theories of authorship.

Evidence cited in support of the traditional view of Zechariah as author of the entire book includes the following: the same priestly background is noticeable throughout the book (Zech. 3:1-8 and 14:16-21); the same stress on the importance of forgiveness of sin (3:1 and 13:1); the same universality of salvation (2:14 ff. and 14:16 ff.); the same picture of the Messiah and His royal priesthood (6:9-15 and 9:9 ff.); some of the same expressions that are somewhat rare and unusual elsewhere in the Scriptures, e.g., "passed through nor returned" (7:14 and 9:8); "eyes of Jahweh" (4:10 and 12:4).

Zechariah has been called "one of the most comforting of all the prophets" (Martin Luther). He gives some broad general Messianic prophecies, cf. Zech. 3:9: "remove guilt"; 6:12: "the man whose name is the Branch"; 8:22: "nations shall come to seek the Lord"; 13:1: "a fountain opened for the house of David"; 14:9: "the Lord will become king over all the earth." He also provides specific prophecies that have New Testament fulfillment recorded: the Palm Sunday entry of Jesus into Jerusalem, Zech. 9:9 f. (Matt. 21:5); payment for Judas' betrayal, Zech. 11:12, 13 (Matt. 26:14; 27:9, 10); piercing of Jesus' side, Zech. 12:10 (John 19:37); smiting of the Shepherd, Zech. 13:7 (Matt. 26:31). These references establish canonicity of the book and support the traditional Jewish and Christian church position in reference to its unity.

A very brief outline of the book is this: eight night visions, Zech. 1—6; a question answered by admonition and promise, 7—8; the Messiah and His kingdom, 9—14.

Someone has suggested that the night visions can be understood best when two lights are focused upon them—the light of the cross and the light of the crown. The Messiah is also pictured in His two states: humiliation and exaltation. To ignore either leads to confusion and misunderstanding of Christ's person and work. Vision I: the angel's four horsemen (Judah cast out but watched over by God), Zech. 1:7-17; Vision II: four horns and four smiths (enemies of Judah overthrown), 1:18-21; Vision III: the measuring line (expansion and prosperity of the city of God), 2:1-13; Vision IV: attiring of Jeshua before Satan (God cleanses His own from sin), 3:1-10; Vision V: the golden candlesticks and the olive trees (God's people, especially His anointed ones, are light-bearers in the world), 4:1-14; Vision VI: the flying roll (the wicked are cursed), 5:1-4; Vision VII: the woman in an ephah (wickedness is removed), 5:5-11; Vision VIII: the four chariots (God's messengers administering righteousness), 6:1-8. The rest of chapter 6 describes the crowning of the high priest in a symbolic act pointing forward to the Messiah in whom the office of priest and king will be united, 6:9-15.

A deputation from Bethel approached Zechariah with a question about fasting and mourning. God responded with an earnest admonition exhorting to deeds of mercy and love with the promise of blessings of joy and feasting. Then He could foresee Gentiles saying to the Jews: "Let us go with you, for we have heard that God is with you," Zech. 7:1—8:23.

The last chapters are replete with prophecies of the coming Messiah and the establishment of a worldwide kingdom. The Messiah will come as a humble man to establish a kingdom of peace, Zech. 9:1-17; and God will equip the church to help in the extension of the kingdom, 10:1-12. The Messiah is portrayed as a Good Shepherd who comes to save but is rejected, 11:1-17. When God visits His people with affliction, they repent and God forgives and blesses, 12:1-12. A fountain is opened to cleanse the people, 13:1-6. Judgment is pronounced upon all the wicked enemies of the Lord but those who honor and enthrone the Lord as King will be blessed forever, 14:1-20.

The Book of Esther

Through the prophetic activity of Haggai and Zechariah and the practical leadership of Jeshua and Zerubbabel the temple reconstruction was completed in 516 B.C. For the next sixty years the Jews who had returned no doubt reclaimed the land and secured their position in Jerusalem and in the surrounding area. The Scriptures give us no report of these years, 516 B.C. to 456 B.C.

This was, however, a period in world history when men, not mentioned in Scripture, made important contributions to world culture and thought which still influence society today. In some instances the exact lifespan of these men is difficult to determine, but the most accurate data available places them in this time period. These are a few of these prominent individuals: Buddha (563—483 B.C.), the respected and idolized leader of meditation in India; Confucius (551—479 B.C.), the sage of China; Phidias (born ca. 500 B.C.), master sculptor of the Parthenon; Herodotus (born ca. 500 B.C.), the "father of history"; Pericles (490—429 B.C.), the Athenian statesman of the "golden age" of democracy; Thucydides (ca. 471—400 B.C.), the first of "scientific" historians; Socrates (470—399 B.C.), the moral philosopher of Greece and the paragon of Plato (427—347 B.C.), the founder of the Academy school of philosophy; and Aeschylus (525—456 B.C.), Greek tragic poet and dramatist.

The only Biblical story in this period occurred far away from Jerusalem among the Jews who had remained in the land of exile. It is the story of Esther and King Ahasuerus (Xerxes I) in 478 B.C. This date is determined by the reference in Esther 2:16, which relates that Esther became queen in the seventh year of the reign of Ahasuerus. The reign of Xerxes extended from 485 B.C. to 465 B.C. Herodotus reports that Xerxes suffered a disastrous defeat by the Greek fleet in 480 B.C.

Many modern Bible scholars categorically reject the Book of Esther as a historical account. Some regard it as religious fiction and others refer to it as a secular legend. Many assume it was written by a loyal Jew to provide an acceptable background for the popular Jewish festival of Purim, still celebrated by Jews all over the world in the middle of March.

Some of the reasons advanced for discounting the historicity of the story are the following: the strange and apparent "symmetrically contrived coincidences"; some historical improbabilities; the total absence of the names of Vashti and Esther as wives of any Persian kings

(Xerxes' wife was Amestris); supposed exaggerations, e.g., 75,000 people killed by the Jews, Esther 9:16; a gallows 75 feet high, 5:14; Haman's bribe of 10,000 talents, $18,000,000, 3:9; and God's name never occurs in the original Hebrew text.

Evidently this latter problem troubled the Jews, and as a result a number of additions to the Hebrew text appear in the Greek translation, the Septuagint, at various places thoughout the book. In these additions the name of God is used profusely. Jerome in his Latin translation, the Vulgate, places these additions as separate chapters at the end of the book (Esther 11—16). Protestants have included them as a separate book among the Apocrypha under the title: "The Additions to the Book of Esther."

A number of the questions and objections concerning the historicity of the Book of Esther can be satisfactorily answered, e.g., the Bible is filled with accounts of providential acts of God that appear to be "symmetrically contrived coincidences"; the most frequently quoted historical improbability is the seeming implication of Esther 2:5, 6 that Mordecai was taken captive with King Jeconiah in 597 B.C., but the text does not necessarily state that; and the supposed exaggerations could well be factual. The reader, interested in further exploration of these issues, is encouraged to consult the books listed in the bibliography.

The author of the book is not known. On the basis of Esther 9:20, 32 some have mentioned Mordecai as the writer, but 9:19 makes that assumption improbable. Ezra is a more likely choice but also that cannot be established. The Jewish historian Josephus and the Babylonian Talmud report that the ancient Jewish church regarded the Book of Esther as an authentic part of the Hebrew Canon. Some of the Jewish scholars, however, questioned its canonicity because of the absence of God's name. The great church father Athanasius also expressed doubt about its canonicity; Martin Luther likewise made some drastic comments about it. Many other Christian scholars through the centuries, while affirming the canonicity, have not accepted it as an accurate historical account. Some raise serious objection to an apparent condoning and even approval of a spirit of revenge on the part of the Jews. Another objection refers to seeming evidence of dishonesty in Esther since she did not immediately reveal her Jewish identity to Ahasuerus. Her character is also impugned because she did not correct the wrong impression Ahasuerus gained that Haman attempted sexual assault. These objections must be evaluated in the light of God's judgment on the wicked in the total context of the Scripture. The Book of Esther strongly corroborates the great theme of the Old Testament: God loved the Jews and determined to preserve them from extinction or annihilation. Likewise the book gives a telling illustration of the truth so frequently emphasized thoughout Scripture: "Cast all your anxieties on Him, for He cares about you," 1 Peter 5:7.

The book revolves around three feasts and their consequences: the feast of Ahasuerus, Esther 1—4; the feast of Esther, 5—8; the feast of Purim, 9—10. The narrative moves along at a lively pace from one exciting event to another. One can understand the moving impact it had, and still has, as it is read at the annual Purim festival celebrating Jewish loyalty and gratitude.

This more detailed outline will be helpful to the reader of the book: Part I: Danger of Annihilation of the Jews, Esther 1:1—5:14: A. The background and origin of the danger: replacement of the rejected Queen Vashti by a beautiful Jewish girl, Esther (Persian word for "star"; her Hebrew name was Hadassah, "myrtle," or "bride"), 1:1—2:18; the report by Mordecai (Esther's cousin and foster-father) of an assassination plot against Ahasuerus, 2:19-23; disrespect toward Haman, the prime minister (an Amalekite, cf. Saul's failure to annihilate the Amalekites,

1 Sam. 15:1-33), on the part of Mordecai, 3:1-6; plot of Haman to kill all Jews, 3:7-15. B. The climax of the danger: great mourning among the Jews at the king's edict, 4:1-3; appeal of Mordecai to Esther, who has "come to the kingdom for such a time as this," 4:4-17; Esther's courage and self-sacrifice in her appearance before King Ahasuerus, 5:1-8; Haman's wicked plot against Mordecai, 5:9-14. . . . Part II: God's Gracious Protection of His People, 6:1—10:3: A. Haman's downfall, King Ahasuerus learns of Mordecai's report of the assassination plot and rewards him, 6:1-14; Esther reveals Haman to King Ahasuerus as a wicked enemy of the Jews, 7:1-10; B. The rescue of the Jews: promotion of Mordecai, 8:1-2; Jews receive official permission from Ahasuerus to defend themselves against any attempt to kill them on the day appointed for their annihilation by Haman, 8:3-13; as the good news spreads, the Jews rejoice, 8:14-17; instead of being annihilated on the 13th day of Adar (ca. March 13), the date Haman had set by casting lots (Purim, 3:7), the Jews kill 75,000 of their enemies, 9:1-19; in gratitude the festival of Purim is inaugurated, 9:20-32; Mordecai is promoted to next in rank to Ahasuerus and becomes a hero to the Jews, "for he sought the welfare of his people and spoke peace to all his people," 10:1-3.

The Book of Nehemiah

The successor of King Ahasuerus (Xerxes I) to the throne of Persia was Artaxerxes I (also called Artaxerxes Longimanus, 465—424 B.C.). Ezra came to Jerusalem in the seventh year of Artaxerxes (ca. 458 B.C.), cf. Ezra 7:7, and Nehemiah came in the twentieth year (ca. 445 B.C.); cf. Neh. 2:1. Questions have been raised about this chronology because some scholars have adduced the following indications that Nehemiah preceded Ezra: Nehemiah includes a list of the Jewish returnees under Jeshua and Zerubbabel but not of those who returned with Ezra; when Nehemiah arrives in Jerusalem, the city is sparsely populated and the walls are broken down, whereas Ezra seems to find Jerusalem thriving—with the walls rebuilt (cf. Ezra 9:9); the high priest contemporary to Nehemiah is Eliashib but Ezra's is Eliashib's grandson, Jehohanan. Since there was another Persian king with the name Artaxerxes (Artaxerxes II Mnemon) who ruled from 404 to 358 B.C., many Bible scholars today place Ezra's arrival after Nehemiah at 397 B.C. This latter position poses problems in reference to the cooperative activity of Nehemiah and Ezra in effecting reforms among the people. The historicity of Nehemiah and Ezra has not been challenged. Scholars agree that both of these men lived and worked as the Scriptures report. Many assume that Nehemiah and Ezra recorded their experiences and activities as personal memoirs which were later incorporated by an unknown author designated as "The Chronicler" in a composite manuscript including the four books presently known as 1 and 2 Chronicles, Ezra, and Nehemiah. Interested readers may want to investigate these assumptions more extensively by consulting some of the suggested readings in the bibliography. The canonicity of the book is universally accepted and, therefore, the Christian reader can find strong motivation for self-sacrificing service after the example of Nehemiah in this inspired book of Scripture.

Nehemiah ("Jahweh has comforted") is distinguish-ed from other Biblical personalities with the same name (cf. Ezra 2:2; Neh. 7:17; Neh. 3:16) by identifying him as "the son of Hachaliah," Neh. 1:1; 10:1. There are indications (Neh. 2:3, 5; 6:6, 7) that Hachaliah was of noble Jewish birth and perhaps of the lineage of David. Nehemiah was employed in the court of Artaxerxes as the royal cupbearer (1:11), a responsible position to protect the king from potential poisoning.

Nehemiah's brother, Hanani, and other concerned Jews reported to Nehemiah at Shushan (Susa), the winter fortress of the Persian kings, that serious problems troubled the Jews in Jerusalem. Nehemiah showed immediate concern and requested permission from Artaxerxes for a leave of absence to go to Jerusalem. The request was granted, and Nehemiah succeeded in leading the Jews to rebuild the walls of Jerusalem in 52 days. He then joined with Ezra, the priest, in instituting renewal of proper worship services, restoration of other covenant obligations, and reform of improper marriage practices. Nehemiah returned to the Persian court, but in 432 B.C. (Neh. 13:6, 7) he secured another leave of absence and resumed his activities of reform in Jerusalem. Nehemiah can serve as an inspiring example to lay leaders in church and community affairs: sincere concern; fervent prayer; accurate information; cooperative planning; courageous persistence; self-sacrificing service; and principled reform.

The book easily divides into two major parts: Nehemiah's trip to Jerusalem and successful rebuilding of the walls, Neh. 1—7; Nehemiah's and Ezra's joint efforts in the restoration of proper worship practices and in renewal of correct covenant living, Neh. 8—13.

The following more complete outline can assist in guiding the reader through the book: Part I: Restoration of the Walls of Jerusalem, Neh. 1:1—7:73: A. Commission to restore the walls: Nehemiah's concern and prayer, 1:1-11; his request to go to Jerusalem, 2:1-8; his journey and personal investigation, 2:9-16; his challenge to the Jews, 2:17-20. B. Work of restoration: names and assignments of builders, 3:1-32; opposition from non-Jewish enemies, 4:1-23; difficulties among the Jews because of greed, 5:1-19; compromise offers and conspiracy by non-Jewish enemies, 6:1-19; completion of walls and registration of the people, 7:1-73.

Part II: Reformation of the People of Jerusalem, Neh. 8:1—13:31. A. Positive reforms: reading and explanation of the Torah (note especially 8:8), 8:1-12;

celebration of the Feast of Tabernacles, 8:13-18; renewal of the covenant, 9:1—10:39; systematic distribution of the people by casting lots, 11:1-36; catalog of priests and Levites who had returned from exile, 12:1-26; dedication of the rebuilt walls, 12:27-43; appointment of treasurers, singers, and porters, 12:44-47. B. Negative reforms, removal of abuses: separating Jews from the "mixed multitude," 13:1-3; Nehemiah's return to Jerusalem and removal from the temple of the furniture of Tobiah, the enemy, 13:4-9; restoration of tithe offerings to the Levites, 13:10-14; curbing of Sabbath breakers, 13:15-22; removal of all heathen spouses, 13:23-31. The prayer of Nehemiah in the last verse of the book may well be repeated by any faithful servant of the Lord: "Remember me, O my God, for good."

The Book of Malachi

It is obvious that the Book of Malachi, with its prophecy of Elijah, Mal. 4:5 (John the Baptist, Matt. 11:10, 14) as the forerunner of the Messiah, is the last of the prophetical books of the Old Testament. It is not so obvious who this prophet was because no biographical information is supplied in the Scripture. A number of Bible scholars do not consider "Malachi" ("My messenger") to be the name of a man but rather an anonymous designation of a prophet to whom the descriptive term "Malachi" was attached in view of the prophecy, 3:1: "Behold, I send My messenger to prepare the way before Me."

Likewise, no specific time indication is given in the book concerning the period in which the prophet lived. There are, however, some hints: the temple has been rebuilt, Mal. 3:10; a governor is ruling, 1:8; many of the same religious and moral defects of Nehemiah's time (laxity in tithes and offerings, improper marriages) are prevalent. Accordingly, it seems that Malachi was a contemporary of Nehemiah and may even have helped to prepare the way for some of the reforms which were effected under Nehemiah. Both the genuineness and the canonicity of the Book of Malachi are unquestioned. These New Testament quotations establish and corroborate the same: Matt. 11:10, 14 (Mal. 4:5); Matt. 17:12 (Mal. 4:5); Mark 1:2 (Mal. 3:1); Mark 9:13 (Mal. 4:5); Luke 1:17 (Mal. 4:5, 6); Rom. 9:13 (Mal. 1:2, 3).

The book comprises two major sections: I. God's love remains unrequited by profane priests and adulterous people, Mal. 1:1—2:17. II. God's call for repentance and conversion is proclaimed to prepare the people for the advent of the Messiah, 3:1—4:5.

The form of the book is different from most of the other prophetical books. Rather than recording a series of sermons or discourses it presents and answers rhetorical questions. With that pattern of questions and answers in mind, the reader can follow this outline in reading the book: God speaking through the prophet assures His people of His love, but in response the people sneeringly ask, "How hast Thou loved us?" God reminds them of the distinction He made between Jacob (the Jews) and Esau (the Edomites), Mal. 1:1-5. Then God asks, "If then I am a Father where is My honor?" This question indicts the priests for their improper sacrifices, 1:6—2:9. Next a question is addressed to the people, "Have we not all one Father? Hath not one God created us? Why then are we faithless to one another?" The answer: "Because they are unfaithful to God, they are also unfaithful to one another, even in marriage," 2:10-17.

When God announces that His messenger will prepare the way and then He will suddenly come, the question is raised, "Who can endure the day of His coming?" God answers that though He will be "like a refiner's fire and like fuller's soap," He loves them and comes to bless, Mal. 3:1-6. God invites them to return to Him and the people ask, "How shall we return?" God responds with a question, "Will man rob God?" The people ask, "How are we robbing Thee?" God points to the lack of proper tithes and offerings but also here adds a generous promise, 3:7-12. A final question to God by the people: "How have we spoken against Thee?" God reveals their laxity and weariness in service to Him, but once again He seeks to motivate them with a beautiful promise of eternal blessing, 3:13-18.

The book closes with a proclamation of the striking contrast that will be evident, "when the day comes," between the evildoers and those who "fear My name." For the latter there is a message of hope: "The Sun of righteousness shall shine with healing in its wings." For the former there is a stern warning to prepare for "the great and terrible day" when God will send Elijah, the prophet (John the Baptist, Matt. 11:10, 14) Mal. 4:1-5.

Malachi stands on the threshold of four hundred years of prophetic silence between the Old and New Testament revelations. God's people will have His Word spoken and written by Moses and the prophets in the previous century, but no new message will be given them by God until, as Malachi prophesies, the great forerunner of the Messiah will appear, John the Baptist, who will prepare the way for Him. He is the capstone of the Old Covenant and the cornerstone of the New, the Alpha and the Omega, the beginning and the end, the first and the last, even Jesus Christ, Son of God and Son of Man, Savior of the world, King of kings and Lord of lords forever!

Appendix I
The Kings and Prophets

JUDAH		Prophets			ISRAEL	
Rehoboam	(17)	Shemaiah		Ahijah	Jeroboam	(22)
Abijah	(3)				Nadab	(2)
Asa	(41)	Azariah			Baasha	(24)
		Hanani			Elah	(2)
		Jehu			Zimri	(7d)
					Omri	(12)
					Ahab	(22)
			Elijah			
Jehoshaphat	(25)	Jahaziel	Micaiah	"	Ahaziah	(2)
		Eliezer	Elisha	"	Jehoram	(12)
Jehoram	(8)	*Obadiah*	"			
Ahaziah	(1)		"		Jehu	(28)
Athaliah	(7)	(Jehoiada)	"			
Joash	(40)	Zechariah	"		Jehoahaz	(17)
		Joel			Jehoash	(16)

Kings of Judah (yrs.)	Prophets of Judah	Prophets	Prophet	Kings of Israel (yrs.)
Amaziah (29)				Jeroboam II (41)
Uzziah (52)		*Amos*	*Jonah*	
		Hosea	*"*	Zachariah (6m)
		"		Shallum (1m)
		"		Menahem (10)
	Isaiah	*"*		Pekahiah (2)
Jotham (16)	*"*			Pekah (20)
Ahaz (16)	*"*	Oded		
	"			Hoshea (9)
Hezekiah (29)	*Micah*			Fall of Samaria 722
Manasseh (55)	*Nahum*			
Amon (2)	*"*			
Josiah (31)	*Habakkuk*			
	Zephaniah			
	Huldah			
	Jeremiah (Lamentations)			
Jehoahaz (3m)	*"*	*Daniel*		
Jehoiakim (11)	*"*	*"*		
Jehoiachin (3m)	*"*	*"*	*Ezekiel*	
Zedekiah (11)	*"*	*"*	*"*	

Fall of Jerusalem 586 B.C.

Restoration—536 B.C.

After the Restoration Haggai/Zechariah 520, Malachi 400 B.C.

Appendix II
Overview of Old Testament
Messianic Prophecy

The entire Old Testament is a development of the one theme that the Son of God will come to earth to redeem the *world* from sin. The first assertion of this is made when God tells the serpent in the presence of Adam and Eve that the seed of the woman will bruise the serpent's, or rather the devil's head. Thereafter the prophecies become more and more explicit. God chose the *Hebrew people*, descendants of Abraham, for this specific purpose. Out of them came the Messiah, the One through whom all the peoples of the earth should be blessed. Thus the Hebrew people are the center of Old Testament history, the ones with whom God makes His *covenant.* Through Jacob, the grandson of Abraham, God narrowed the Messianic prophecy to the *tribe of Judah.* Four hundred years later God said through Moses that it would be "Another Prophet" like unto him. The whole system of Jewish sacrifices also pointed to the coming sacrifice which the Messiah was to bring for the sins of the world.

One thousand years after God spoke to Abraham, He narrowed the prophecy still more by saying that from the tribe of Judah it would be the *family of David.* From that time on to the close of the Old Testament, the central interest is in David's family. The first form that God's covenant promise to David took was the promise of an *eternal throne* for David and his family. Then came a long line of prophets, explaining that the promises to the Davidic family of an everlasting dynasty would find their culmination in One Great King, who Himself would live forever and establish an *everlasting kingdom.* The *Psalms of David* abound in hints and prophecies of the coming King:

His deity, His humiliation and suffering, His resurrection, His eternal priesthood, His conquering might, His endless universal righteous reign, and the immortal bliss of His redeemed people.

Two hundred years later, *Joel* paints a beautiful picture of the Gospel age when by the Holy Spirit people from every nation would be brought to God. About this time *Jonah* was sent on his errand of mercy to Nineveh. Earlier *Obadiah* had prophesied the doom of Edom because it opposed Israel, God's chosen people. *Amos,* when the throne of David was falling and when it looked as if God's promises were coming to naught, insisted that the kingdom would be revived and yet be supreme in the world. *Hosea,* about the same time, in the days of Israel's apostasy (adultery), was certain a remnant of Israel would remain true and God would be acknowledged by Gentiles also.

Isaiah, three hundred years after David, when David's kingdom lay low, prophesied that the family of David would persist and a Wonderful Child would be born who would inherit the throne of David. As Jehovah's Servant, He would endure severe humiliation and suffering for man, and then live and rule forever. *Micah,* contemporary with Isaiah, said the Wonderful Child would be born in Bethlehem.

About a hundred years later, *Nahum* comforted God's people by announcing the doom of Nineveh. *Zephaniah* announced judgment on a number of idolatrous nations but promised a remnant of Judah would be hid by God and saved. *Habakkuk* was certain Jehovah's glory would yet cover the earth, though all seemed dark at that time. *Jeremiah,* while David's kingdom was falling and God's people were being scattered, announced that God's promises are irrevocable. Therefore the covenant with David could not be broken, and God would yet accomplish through the family of David what He said He would through the Righteous Branch to be born into that family.

Ezekiel, in a foreign land, justified to the captive people the ways of God in permitting the captivity and saw visions of a reborn nation, an ideal King and an ideal temple, symbolizing the Savior and the New Testament church. *Daniel,* contemporary with Ezekiel, counselor to the kings of Babylon and

Persia, predicted the course of empires from his days to the time when the "Anointed One," the Prince, would appear. *Haggai* and *Zechariah*, back again in Jerusalem, urged the people to rebuild the temple and pointed forward to the far grander House of God (New Testament church) to be built by the coming Davidic King, the "desire of nations." Zechariah abounded in specific Messianic prophecies. *Malachi* closed the Old Testament by stating that the Messiah would be ushered in by a prophet like Elijah.

The Old Testament: Book by Book

GENESIS: Creation; flood; Abraham; Isaac; Jacob; Joseph.

EXODUS: Israel called out of Egypt and consecrated.

LEVITICUS: Sacrifices; priesthood; purifications; festivals.

NUMBERS: Israel's journey from Sinai to Moab.

DEUTERONOMY: Moses' farewell rehearsal of Jewish laws and history.

JOSHUA: The conquest and division of Canaan.

JUDGES: Alternate oppressions and deliverances in first years in Canaan.

RUTH: Beginning of Messianic family of David: Boaz-Ruth-Obed-Jesse.

1 SAMUEL: Israel under Samuel, Saul, and David.

2 SAMUEL: The reign of David.

1 KINGS: The reign of Solomon and division of the kingdom.

2 KINGS: History of the kingdoms of Israel and Judah.

1 CHRONICLES: The reign of David.

2 CHRONICLES: History of the Southern Kingdom (Judah).

EZRA: Return from the Captivity; building the temple; reforms.

NEHEMIAH: Rebuilding the walls of Jerusalem.

ESTHER: Escape of Jews, by God's providence, from extermination.

JOB: Enduring suffering under critical analysis in the hope of a Redeemer.

PSALMS: National hymnbook of God's people (150 psalms).

PROVERBS: Collection of moral and religious maxims.

ECCLESIASTES: Vanity of earthly life without fear of God.

SONG OF SOLOMON: Wedded love as symbol of God's love for the church.

ISAIAH: Messianic prophet: Jehovah is Salvation.

JEREMIAH: God's final effort to save Jerusalem by this martyr prophet.

LAMENTATIONS: A dirge over desolation of Jerusalem.

EZEKIEL: "They shall know that I am God." Justifies God's action upon Judah.

DANIEL: The kingdoms of the world and the kingdom of God.

HOSEA: Apostasy from God is spiritual adultery.

JOEL: Locust plague; repentance; Gospel age of Holy Spirit.

AMOS: Judgments on Gentile nations and Israel. David's house will rule.

OBADIAH: Edom doomed because of opposition to Israel.

JONAH: God's mercy knows no boundaries (Nineveh).

MICAH: Bethlehem the birthplace of the Messiah for all people.

NAHUM: Destructive vengeance on Nineveh.

HABAKKUK: Judah invaded; Chaldea doomed; just shall live by faith.

ZEPHANIAH: Searching judgments of God. The remnant "hid by God."

HAGGAI: "Build ye the house of the Lord."

ZECHARIAH: The house of the Lord and its glorious future in New Testament church.

MALACHI: Final message to a disobedient people (Elijah—John the Baptist).

Appendix III
Messianic Prophecy

Prophecies of a Kingly Messiah
Ps. 2:6-8; Ps. 68:18; Ps. 118:22; Is. 9:6, 7; Is. 32:1-3; Is. 42:1-4;
Jer. 23:5; Dan. 2:44; Dan. 7:13, 14; Micah 5:2; Zech. 6:12, 13;
Zech. 9:9, 10; Mal. 3:1.

Prophecies of a Suffering Messiah
Ps. 69:21; Ps. 22:18; Is. 50:6; Is. 52:14; Is. 53:1-10; Dan. 9:26;
Zech. 11:12; Zech. 12:10; Zech. 13:7

Prophecies		*Fulfillment*
Gen. 3:15	Would be the "Seed of a Woman"	Gal. 4:4
Gen. 18:18	Promised Seed of Abraham	Acts 3:25
Gen. 17:19	Promised Seed of Isaac	Matt. 1:2
Num. 24:17	Promised Seed of Jacob	Luke 3:34
Gen. 49:10	Will Descend from the Tribe of Judah	Luke 3:33
Is. 9:7	The Heir to the Throne of David	Matt. 1:1
Micah 5:2	Place of Birth	Matt. 2:1
Dan. 9:25	Time of Birth	Luke 2:1, 2
Is. 7:14	Born of a Virgin	Matt. 1:18
Jer. 31:15	Massacre of Infants	Matt. 2:16
Hos. 11:1	Flight into Egypt	Matt. 2:14
Is. 9:1, 2	Ministry in Galilee	Matt. 4:12-16
Deut. 18:15	As a Prophet	John 6:14

Prophecies		*Fulfillment*
Ps. 110:4	As a Priest, like Melchizedek	Heb. 6:20
Is. 53:3	His Rejection by Jews	John 1:11
Is. 11:2	Some of His Characteristics	Luke 2:52
Zech. 9:9	His Triumphal Entry	John 12:13, 14
Ps. 41:9	Betrayed by a Friend	Mark 14:10
Zech. 11:12	Sold for Thirty Pieces of Silver	Matt. 26:15
Zech. 11:13	Money to be Returned for a Potter's Field	Matt. 27:6, 7
Ps. 109:7, 8	Judas' Office to Be Taken by Another	Acts 1:18-20
Ps. 27:12	False Witnesses Accuse Him	Matt. 26:60, 61
Is. 53:7	Silent When Accused	Matt. 26:62, 63
Is. 50:6	Smitten and Spat Upon	Mark 14:65
Ps. 69:4	Was Hated Without a Cause	John 15:23-25
Is. 53:4, 5	Suffered Vicariously	Matt. 8:16, 17
Is. 53:12	Crucified with Sinners	Matt. 27:38
Ps. 22:16	Hands and Feet Pierced	John 20:27
Ps. 22:6-8	Mocked and Insulted	Matt. 27:39, 40
Ps. 69:21	Given Gall and Vinegar	John 19:29
Ps. 22:8	Hears Prophetic Words Repeated in Mockery	Matt. 27:43
Ps. 109:4	Prays for His Enemies	Luke 23:34
Zech. 12:10	His Side to Be Pierced	John 19:34
Ps. 22:18	Soldiers Cast Lots for His Coat	Mark 15:24
Ps. 34:20	Not a Bone to Be Broken	John 19:33
Is. 53:9	To Be Buried with the Rich	Matt. 27:57-60
Ps. 16:10	His Resurrection	Matt. 28:9
Ps. 68:18	His Ascension	Luke 24:50, 51

Appendix IV
The History and Literature
of the Old Testament

God begins the Bible with the book of *Genesis*. He tells us of the creation of the world in perfection but also of its corruption by the devil's rebellion against God and Adam's and Eve's falling into sin. Immediately God announced a plan of salvation for all mankind. Later He called Abraham to be the "father of the faithful," i.e., the first of the covenant people, who would keep the covenant message alive and through whom the Messiah would come. This did not mean that the covenant people would have no sorrow and trouble in this world. This is demonstrated already in the early story of the afflictions of *Job*. Abraham's descendants were led to Egypt through a famine and remained there in slavery until God led them out in the mighty *Exodus* under Moses to Mt. Sinai, where He formed a permanent, specific covenant with these children of Abraham. Thereafter, they carried the name of Abraham's grandson, Jacob or Israel. *Leviticus* contains the plan of sacrifice, discipline, and worship which God revealed to His people! By this plan they could continue the covenant relationship. *Numbers* contains the account of the beginning of the journey toward Canaan and how Israel's rebellion caused the journey to stretch into forty years and how God prepared the second generation of covenant people for entry into Canaan. In *Deuteronomy* we hear the farewell addresses of Moses and read of his death just before the covenant people enter into Canaan.

Joshua demonstrates how in obedience to the covenant, the people possessed the covenant land and divided it among the twelve tribes. In the book of *Judges* we see a falling away from the covenant through idolatry and God's calling the people back through the attack of enemies and delivering them through "judges" or "deliverers." *Ruth,* great-grandmother of David, was a Moabitess who came to Bethlehem.

In *1 Samuel* we are told how the people returned to a worship of the true God under Samuel but then became more and more "like the nations" in that they demanded and got a king, whose name was Saul. *2 Samuel* tells of the rule of David, the golden age of covenant history. The kingdom flourished and the worship life of the covenant people was enriched with the writing of many *Psalms,* of which David wrote at least 73. *1 Chronicles* reviews the spiritual history of God's covenant people from Adam to David. The first part of *1 Kings* gives the history of the United Kingdom under Solomon, who led the building of the temple. The first part of *2 Chronicles* also gives interesting details about Solomon's reign and the building of the temple. It was at this time that covenant philosophy was presented in three books written by Solomon. In the book of *Proverbs* we have a large number of maxims which emphasize the importance of living, especially also in youth, in the fear of God. This will cause covenant people to avoid the fatalistic and frustrating philosophy of seeking after the "vanity" of this world, as pictured in *Ecclesiastes.* In the *Song of Solomon* the beauty of the loving covenant relation between God and Israel is presented under the picture of wedded love.

Solomon was extremely rich but had also taxed his people heavily, and his son, Rehoboam, refused to change the situation. Thus the ten tribes of the north split away under Jeroboam, and two kingdoms were formed. The history of the Divided Kingdom is contained in *1 and 2 Kings.* More details, particularly about Judah and the Southern Kingdom, are given in *2 Chronicles.* Idolatry spread widely throughout both kingdoms. Many of the kings of Judah and all the kings of Israel were wicked and idolatrous and "like the nations." But God was merciful, and for almost 500 years continued to send His prophets to warn the people against breaking the covenant and promising them blessings if they would remain true to him. A "remnant" always did.

The first of the writing prophets was *Obadiah,* who announced the destruction of Edom, Esau's descendants. A little later came *Joel,* who announced the judgment of God upon His covenant people through a plague of locusts but also promised the marvelous outpouring of the Holy Spirit in the New Testament. At the time when Jeroboam II was king of the Northern Kingdom, *Jonah* was sent by God to Nineveh in Assyria to call it to repentance. At this same time *Amos,* a farmer, brought God's messages against the social sins of Israel and Judah and the surrounding nations. *Hosea* prophesied shortly thereafter and continued to plead with the covenant people to return to the love of God until the Northern Kingdom was utterly destroyed. Then God sent *Micah* to warn both the leaders and the people that sin would bring judgment. Micah also announced that the Messiah would be born in Bethlehem. The greatest of the prophets, *Isaiah,* lived at this time. In the first part of his writings he speaks very sharply against the sins of Judah but in the last part brings most beautiful promises of the Messiah and His kingdom in the New Testament. Shortly thereafter the prophet *Nahum* announces that God will utterly destroy Nineveh and Assyria and at the same time the prophet *Zephaniah* tells the covenant people that in the "day of wrath" God will hide His covenant people and keep them safe. Then the prophet *Habakkuk* announces that God will use the Chaldeans (Babylonians) to punish Judah, but then He will also visit His punishment upon the Chaldeans. Habakkuk also announces that the just who remain faithful to the covenant shall live. God's earnest attempt to save Jerusalem and Judah from captivity shows itself in the earnest preaching of *Jeremiah,* but the people refused to listen. In 586 B.C. Jerusalem was taken and many Jews were carried to Babylon. Jeremiah mourns this in *Lamentations.*

Even in the captivity God did not forsake His people. Here we find the prophet *Ezekiel* defending God's action to the people and urging them to repent and to turn to Him. We see how God's covenant people continue to serve Him by the faithful example of *Daniel.* In the book of the priest *Ezra* we are told of a remnant of Judah returning to Jerusalem to rebuild the temple under Jeshua and Zerubbabel. Since the people in Jerusalem were slow in rebuilding the temple, God sent two prophets to urge them on: *Haggai* emphasized especially the rebuilding of the physical temple, and *Zechariah* emphasized that this physical temple was to be a picture of the building of the spiritual temple in the New Testament. Many Jews remained in the land of captivity, and here we have the comforting story of God's providence in the book of *Esther*, where God saved His people from extermination. In the second part of the book of *Ezra*, named for a priest, we are told how Ezra and a layman, *Nehemiah*, came to Jerusalem about 450 B.C. to urge the covenant people to get back to covenant worship and covenant living. Nehemiah especially led the people in rebuilding the city walls. In *Malachi*, the last book of the Old Testament, we also read of earnest rebukes of the people's sins, especially in not bringing proper offerings to God, but Malachi also announces the coming of the forerunner of the Messiah, John the Baptist.

Thereafter, we have no inspired writings of God for 400 years. A number of books were written to describe this period between Malachi and Matthew, but these were not inspired. They are called *The Apocrypha.*

Selected Bibliography

These are some of the books most frequently consulted in the preparation of this manuscript.

Aaseng, Rolf E. *The Sacred Sixty-Six*. Minneapolis: Augsburg Publishing House, 1967.

Albright, W. F. *The Biblical Period from Abraham to Ezra*. Pittsburgh: Biblical Colloquium, 1950.

American Lutheran Professors. *The Bible: Book of Faith*. Minneapolis: Augsburg Publishing House, 1964.

Anderson, Bernhard W. *Understanding the Old Testament*. Englewood Cliffs, N.J.: Prentice-Hall, Inc., 1966.

Archer, Gleason Jr. *A Survey of Old Testament Introduction*. Chicago: Moody Press, 1972.

Bruce, F. F. *Israel and the Nations*. Grand Rapids: Wm. B. Eerdmans Publishing Co., 1963.

Cornfeld, Gaalyahu. *Adam to Daniel*. New York: The Macmillan Company, 1961.

Fuerbringer, L. F. *Introduction to the Old Testament*. St. Louis: Concordia Publishing House, 1925.

Gottwald, Norman K. *A Light to the Nations*. New York: Harper & Brothers, 1959.

Hahn, Herbert H. *The Old Testament in Modern Research*. Philadelphia: Fortress Press, 1966.

Harrelson, Walter. *Interpreting the Old Testament.* New York: Holt, Rinehart and Winston, Inc., 1964.

Hegland, Martin. *Getting Acquainted with the Bible.* Minneapolis: Augsburg Publishing House, 1953.

Hendricksen, William. *Bible Survey.* Grand Rapids: Baker Book House, 1953.

Huggenvik, Theodore. *Your Key to the Bible.* Minneapolis: Augsburg Publishing House, 1945.

Klinck, A. W. *Old Testament History.* St. Louis: Concordia Publishing House, 1938.

Kuntz, J. Kenneth. *The People of Ancient Israel.* New York: Harper & Row, 1974.

Laetsch, Theo. *The Minor Prophets.* St. Louis: Concordia Publishing House, 1956.

Larue, Gerald A. *Old Testament Life and Literature.* Boston: Allyn and Bacon, Inc., 1968.

Mears, Henrietta C. *What the Bible Is All About.* Glendale, Calif.: Regal Books Division, G/L Publications, 1970.

Milton, John P. *Our Hebrew-Christian Heritage.* Madison, Wis.: Straus Printing and Publishing Co., 1973.

Rupprecht, F. *Bible History References,* Volume I. St. Louis: Concordia Publishing House, 1957.

Schultz, S. J. *The Old Testament Speaks.* New York: Harper & Row, 1960.

Young, Edward J. *An Introduction to the Old Testament.* Grand Rapids: Wm. B. Eerdmans Publishing Co., 1950.

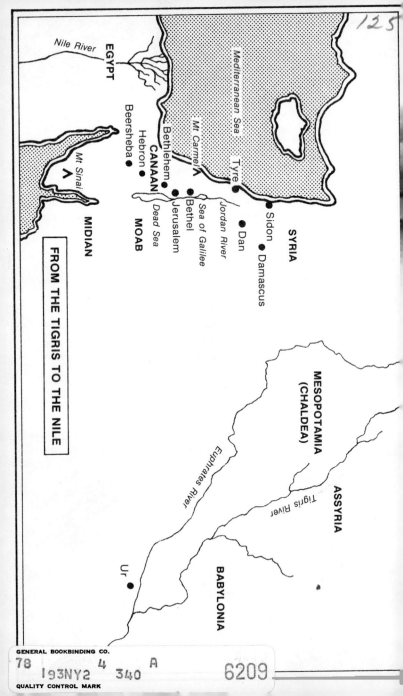

FROM THE TIGRIS TO THE NILE

Nile River

EGYPT

Mediterranean Sea

Mt Sinai

MIDIAN

CANAAN

Beersheba
Hebron
Bethlehem
Jerusalem
Bethel
Mt Carmel
Tyre
Sidon
Dan
Damascus

MOAB

Dead Sea
Sea of Galilee
Jordan River

SYRIA

MESOPOTAMIA
(CHALDEA)

ASSYRIA

Euphrates River

Tigris River

Ur

BABYLONIA

125